Darren,

Just Have Faith +
Keep It Moving!

Just Have

Faith

Thank you for your
Support!

Fanny Minnitt

minnittjusthavefaith@gmail.com

Just Have

Faith

*What to Do When You Cannot
See What You Hope For*

FANNY MINNITT

iUniverse®

JUST HAVE FAITH
WHAT TO DO WHEN YOU CANNOT SEE WHAT YOU HOPE FOR

Unless otherwise indicated, all scriptures are taken from the King James Version of the Bible (KJV). Additional information can be found at https://www.biblegateway.com/versions/King-James-Version-KJV-Bible.com.

iUniverse books may be ordered through booksellers or by contacting:

iUniverse
1663 Liberty Drive
Bloomington, IN 47403
www.iuniverse.com
1-800-Authors (1-800-288-4677)

Artwork in this book is by Artist Luca D. Pearson.

Cover Photos of author taken by Glamour Shots, at Village on the Green, Dallas, Texas, and author's make-up by Ellie.

ISBN: 978-1-4917-7877-7 (sc)
ISBN: 978-1-4917-7876-0 (e)

Library of Congress Control Number: 2015916930

Print information available on the last page.

iUniverse rev. date: 11/16/2015

Contents

Acknowledgments

Thank you, God, for the heavens and the earth and all things that are in it. Thank you, Holy Spirit, for quickening my spirit with creativity, knowledge, wisdom, and favor to write this book.

Thank you, readers, for purchasing my book. Please continue to spread my story and help me to sell this book. I believe it will help others to increase the dialogue about God's amazing grace and faithfulness.

Thank you, Theodore Minnitt Jr., my husband of thirty-two years, and your entire family. To my son, Terrance Y. Minnitt, and my grandson, YulShay Minnitt, you all have inspired me beyond what I can describe. Terrance, when God gave you to me, my life began to change. Min, I love you, man. I pray that every woman who desires a husband is blessed with the kind of love that you give me. You are a great husband. To my brothers and sisters—Sherry, Quinton, Tara, Tonya, Ricky, and Nana—we have created so many memories, and you all have supported me throughout my lifetime. To my cousin Melvin Smith, a.k.a. Butch, I will forever be grateful for you.

Thank you to my friends: Diane Easter, my free counselor for many years; Pat and Ben Law; Violetta Butler; Earlene Franklin; Angela Sumpter; Wanda Reynolds; and Delphine Hopkins; and the other staff at Rancier Middle School. Thank you to Della Ross, owner of Porcelain

Palace, located in Killeen, Texas, and Shanda Scott, master cosmetologist and owner of Gifted Hands Salon in Copperas Cove. (Shanda, I will never forget how you held me and recited Psalm 23 to me minutes after my mother died.) In addition, I thank others for their support and for helping me throughout some of the most difficult and intriguing times in my life.

Thank you to my former neighbors from Sabine Pass in Beaumont, Texas—too many to name. Helen Tegbe Sutton, girl, you know that you have a book to write and a story to tell. Ora D. Johnson Hines, my BFF since the sixth grade, you already know how much I appreciate you.

Thank you to Luca D. Pearson, featured artist, Glamour Shots, and Julie and the wonderful staff at Village on the Green, Dallas, Texas, for an awesome cover picture. Thank you also to iUniverse, a self-publishing company; Wanda Gunter, author of *Broken Silence*; and Linda and J. L. Crawford, owners of *The Anchor News*, Waco, Texas, and the *Killeen Daily Herald*, Killeen, Texas. TBN, please continue to introduce great men and women of God to the world. Tenille Davis, walk in faith, and open that school. Our children need you. And Lindsey Phillips, thank you for helping me to set up my social media. In addition, I thank all the businesses that supported me throughout my ventures and those who are supporting me now.

Thank you to all the church congregations that I have gleaned from throughout my extensive travel. You are so great!

If I did not mention your name or business, it is not because I do not love you or want to thank you. It is because there are so many people who have walked and talked with me throughout my faithful journey that it is impossible for me to continue my list. I truly love the Lord for placing so many people, businesses, and TBN into my life.

Introduction

WHAT TO DO WHEN YOU CANNOT SEE WHAT YOU HOPE FOR

$\mathcal{I}$ have lived in many different states and traveled or lived in other countries. I am a licensed minister; I have a degree in business administration, corporate communication, and education administration. Because of my experiences, I felt compelled to share some things that I learned along my life's journey.

Three years ago, I started to write a book called *Do You Really Want to Be an Entrepreneur?* for those who are contemplating going into business for themselves, those who have started businesses recently, people who have not thought about what it takes to be in business, and those who have been successful and unsuccessful in starting businesses.

I challenged people to ask themselves two questions: "Can my passion bring me profit?" and "Do I really want to be an entrepreneur?" My hope and desire was to finish this book in 2012. I even hired a friend to start the editing process. My goal was to launch it December 15, 2012, and then life happened. I placed this project on the bookshelf in the closet.

Within my heart and soul, I continued to have hopes of one day completing the book. Years later, we moved to Cedar Hill, Texas, and after settling down, I pulled out my manuscript and began reading it. Suddenly something strange happened to me. I stopped reading and instantly lost interest in completing a book that had been wandering around in my memory for months. It had been my dream to produce a book to help others and my retail business. My business closed, and the desire to write my book began to fade away—but not for long.

The words *have faith* started to rush and float across my mind on a pretty ribbon: "Have faith. Have faith. Have faith …" It was so pretty! I returned to normal life and placed my partial manuscript on the shelf in my new home.

I remember preparing to go to bed that night and hearing the words "Have faith" again. I had the craziest dream that night. In it, a well-known jazz musician was standing in front of me and a friend in line at an event that thousands of people were attending. My friend and I were talking about finding a song to go with my book *Have Faith*. The huge crowd parted as he turned around to look at me. Then he stomped his feet and said, "Just have faith." He did this a few times, and then the crowd roared, "Just have faith!" I shouted, "Okay! *Just Have Faith* is what I will name my CD. The trumpet has to be played on this CD, and I hope that my sister Tara is going to sing on the CD as well." I woke up the next morning, grabbed my tape recorder, and recorded what I had heard in my dream. Later I took out a notebook and began writing *Just Have Faith*.

Chapter 1 is about faith, and it gives a brief origin of the meaning of *faith*. The meaning came from revelations during my faith journey. You will also find information regarding others I consider to be faith soldiers. I do not know how they do it, but I ask the Lord all the time to increase my faith.

This chapter, like most of the chapters in this book, begins with several questions. Some of the chapters are short, while other chapters may be lengthy, but they all come straight from my heart. The questions are to get you to think about your life in general. Life is about faith. Before reading an entire chapter, take two or three of the questions and answer them honestly. You may be wondering what the question in the chapter has to do with faith. Can you just have faith?

I mention the definition given in Hebrews 11:1 and a few other references that will explain faith. Ultimately, faith comes by hearing and hearing by the Word of God. For that reason, read the Bible, which was inspired by God. His words are life changing.

Chapter 2 is about my past and my faith journey. I believe that our past dictates how we react to our present and that our present dictates how we respond to our future. We live in a state of hope—hope for now, hope for later. We must learn to hold on to our faith and trust in God. Too often, we give up when we cannot see what we have hoped for.

As for chapter 3, remember I talked about the book I was going to write three years ago? Look at God's mercy and grace. The things I started writing in that book three years ago were for this book in 2015. I am so amazed at the strategic plans that God has for our lives. Do not faint or grow weary about anything that you have not accomplished; every creative thought that is deposited into your spirit, God will use at His appointed time if you just have faith.

Chapter 4 is about my faith and wavering during my mother's battle with dementia and Alzheimer's disease. This was the hardest chapter to write. I was unaware that I still had feelings that needed releasing. I thought it was my mother's battle, but it was mine too. We have to continue to hold on to our faith and believe that God's got it—whatever it is! It will begin to take you out if you do not give it all to God.

Chapter 5 is about Abraham's story, which still fascinates me. In addition, I also talk about how I resigned from my job. I ended up going from being a school administrator to being a substitute teacher, but not by choice. Fortunately stepping out on faith rendered me an unbelievable amount of peace and an increase in my faith walk, not to mention an increase in affluence.

Chapter 6 is about how we treat family matters, how generations are broken, unsettled, and lost because of family matters stemming from years of corrupt communication. We must start pulling our families and friends back together and stop the madness.

In chapter 7, I speak about ministry in general. Too often, we think that we only qualify to minister to people if we are ordained or licensed. Nevertheless, life consists of us ministering to people daily, if we know our purpose on earth. Start giving, helping, and being more involved in helping people to seek after righteousness and understand more about the wonderful gift of faith that God has given us. You are a part of building God's kingdom on earth as it is in heaven. If each one of us does our part, what a wonderful world this would be. Just have faith.

There are illustrations throughout the book, which an artist sketched or painted. A brief description of the meaning of each illustration is given. These illustrations are visuals of my thoughts that were inspired by the Word and my life journey. I am still on a journey, so this is not it.

Always let God order your steps. God is amazing! God is marvelous! When you finish reading this book or while you are reading it, if you have a dream deposited inside of you, get up and get busy. I did. Remember to *just have faith*!

Chapter 1

WHAT IS FAITH?

What do you believe in? Why do you believe what you believe? Do you ever think about what you think about? Who are you? What is your purpose in life? When you leave this earth, where are you going? Do you think that once you die, that is it? Whom do you give to? Whom do you take from? How are you living your life? Are you true to yourself?

These questions entered my mind after I began writing the first chapter of this book. Then I had to ask myself, "Why am I asking so many questions?" Kind of odd, right? I started to take out some of the questions, but they echoed in my spirit for someone who is reading this book. Besides, it is okay; knowing that you have a mind to think and process with is faith.

"Now Faith is the substance of things hoped for, the evidence of things not seen" (Hebrews 11:1). Faith is faith in faith, in trust, and in the trustworthiness of a person, idea, thing, or place. You cannot initially see it, but it is so.

Dr. Frederick K. C. Price wrote one of the best books I have read about faith titled *Faith, Foolishness, or Presumption?*[1] He started by saying, "Faith is a way of life." He shared the scripture Habakkuk 2:4: "Behold, his soul which is lifted up is not upright in him: but the just shall live by his faith." I learned some commonsense things from his book. Bishop T. D. Jakes, senior pastor at The Potter's House in Dallas, Texas offers divine training in biblical studies and practical life skills. I attended a class during the fall of 2009 at the Potter's Institute. Elder Shelia King[2] was the instructor. She talked about how love is the motivator and faith is the activator. She said that faith is the key to accessing the promises in the kingdom of God. I had not heard it spoken this way before. I thought about love equaling to the activation of faith, and of course, I thought about the scripture John 3:16: "For God so loved the world, that he gave his only begotten Son, that whosoever believed in him should not perish, but have everlasting life." God had to have had faith in humanity to take a chance committing such an act of love.

Now faith is not foolishness. Why do I say this? It is because some of you do some crazy things in the name of faith and then you blame your cause and effect on everybody else. Some Christians like to blame God. Stop the madness! They do weird things like stop paying their bills, and when the bill collectors start calling, they throw their hands in the air shouting, "The Lord will make a way!" That's not faith. That's you finding an excuse not to do the right thing. You must pay your debts; paying what you owe is scripture. Now faith is the thing you hope for (e.g., debt going away) and the thing that you, at the time of your issue, cannot see your way out of (e.g., bills totaling $2,450 a month, but your monthly net income totals $2,000). Therefore, if you have overextended yourself or life happened to you, faith would mean believing that no matter how much debt you are in and no matter how much money you make, it will soon be over. Why? Because you first trust in God, while you are actively paying on bills with the few pennies you have. In addition, you have contacted all parties involved to discuss a way to take care of the situation. Even better, you open your mail and an unexpected check for a large sum of money clears all your debt. So do not stop answering the phone. Say, "I trust God; I have faith that this mountain will be moved into the sea."

If your mind starts running away from you, catch it! Selling drugs or your body, using your babies, crawling up in a corner crying, or giving up is not going to resolve your issues; these things are not viable options. Faith will change the outcome of all matters. Believe what you hope for, receive it, and just have faith.

The mountains that I often go to battle with these days are lack of exercising, eating the wrong foods, and excessive shopping. I continue to pray for a complete renewal of the mind regarding these issues. My prayer is that these mountains are in the sea by the release of this book *Just Have Faith*. "It is done" is my faith.

Stop right now. Don't dwell on what I have written so far or on your situation at this time (good or bad). I need you to empty yourself and ask God to increase your, your family's, and your friends' faith in God. Ask Him again for yourself, "God increase my faith in your Word!" Do you have faith that He heard your request? Believe it!

The Bible is the manual to life. Start reading it. You will find that the events in the Old and New Testament parallel the events we are witnessing and experiencing today. I am going to share a couple of stories with you that are in the Bible; observe the characters' incredible faith. The more you know, the more you grow. Oh, what a relief you will encounter! It is a peace that is hard to explain. My first characters are Abraham (Abram) and Sarah (Sarai). I am not going to tell the entire story, so you need to read the story in its entirety later. While you are reading my paraphrasing of Abraham's faith, allow the story to come alive, see the characters, and picture their reactions. Think about how you would have reacted in their situation. Ask yourself, "Do I have that kind of faith?" Alternatively, ask, "How can I develop a closer walk with God so that I may encounter an increase in my faith?"

After Abram's father died (later in the text, God renamed Abram, Abraham, and Sarai, Sarah), the Lord said to him that He would bless Sarah and give her a son and that she would be the mother of nations.

Kings of people would be of her. When Abraham heard this, he fell upon his face and laughed. He said in his heart, "Shall a child be born unto him that is an hundred years old? And shall Sarah, who is ninety years old, bear?" You see, Sarah was infertile. I am not sure about you, but I cannot imagine a one-hundred-year-old man and a ninety-year-old woman having a baby. I cannot imagine them being intimate at that age, other than hugs, kisses, and a little touching or feeling. Therefore, I can understand why Abraham laughed in his heart. Sarah laughed when she heard this news too. I understand the laughter because I am not sure how I would take news like that at my age. The point of this brief information is that after they received the initial shock, they believed it and then received it. It then came to pass.

God's words do not fail. Proverbs 3:5 states, "Trust in the LORD with all thine heart; and lean not unto thine own understanding." Mark 12:30 said, "And thou shalt love the Lord thy God with all thy heart, and with all thy soul, and with all thy mind, and with all thy strength: this [is] the first commandment." We need to trust in the Lord with all our heart, soul, and spirit. If you do not, ask yourself why. You know that love is a gift from God. Ask Him to increase your faith. Just have faith!

Often we write down New Year's resolutions and then wander in the wilderness until the next year happens. You must truly believe in what you say or write down, but there is another step. That step is receiving what you believe and then stepping out on faith (even if you do not see it happening). That is what faith is all about. Faith is the substance of things hoped for and the evidence of things not seen.

I am writing this book and have already paid a self-publishing company to publish the book for me. I haven't even given the company the name of the book or any other information on the book at this time. But I have faith that I will complete the book before I leave this earth and that it is well regarding all circumstances surrounding the completion, the distribution around the world, the book signings, the royalties, and so on, because I have faith. I do not believe that God put this book in my spirit to lie dormant. Only believing would not have produced this book.

I had to do something to birth it. If you have something inside of you, stop analyzing it, asking if it sounds okay, and wondering if it will work. Stop pondering your past failures or your past in general.

Here is another story I have to share with you. In the Bible, there was a woman by the name of Naomi, and she and her family moved far from their home because there was a famine in the land where they resided. They sojourned in the country of Moab. Her sons were married to Moabite women. One of the women was named Ruth and the other Opal. Although they moved to Moab to avoid a famine, the family story ended in tragedy. Naomi's husband and her two sons died. This left Naomi and her two daughters-in-law. I do not know about you, but this would have been a bit much for me. At some point, Naomi decided to return home. She told her two daughters-in-law to stay. Opal kissed her good-bye and got to stepping. However, Ruth saw something in Naomi. She trusted Naomi and wanted to serve Naomi's God. What an impact Naomi's lifestyle had on Ruth!

Do you ever wonder if your lifestyle is affecting others to the point that they want to serve the God that you serve? That people would want to follow you to another city, state, or country? What are you living like? Ultimately, Ruth followed Naomi back to her country. Ruth did not have any idea what would happen to her or Naomi. She just had faith in the things that she could not see. Read the story of Ruth. It is so good. Did I mention that she left her family and friends? God always makes provisions. In Ruth's case, she was blessed abundantly above all that she could have asked or thought of. Take the time right now, and ask God to increase your faith, believe that He will, receive what you ask for, and then walk in your faith!

I am going to leave you with a visual. David represents us in the illustration, and the big mountain represents our Goliaths—debts, illnesses, bad decision making, death, and more. Too often, we feel that we have no control; we feel defeated. Some people give up; some even commit suicide. We must trust that the God we serve will give us whatever we need to take a stone and knock our mountains down. Read the story of David and Goliath again. The story is talking about the same God we serve today. David was a man after God's heart! I am a woman after God's heart too! I am writing to tell you to just have faith.

"So then faith cometh by hearing, and hearing by the word of God" (Romans 10:17). Why am I sharing this scripture with you? You need to pay attention to God's voice. Nevertheless, if you do not know His voice, no telling what you are listening to. Study His word—study, study, study!

You have experienced a mountain, or you know someone who is now experiencing mountains in his or her life. Encourage that person to read the Word and just have faith!

Chapter 2

MY PAST AND FAITH

*D*oes your past have anything to do with how you feel about faith? Did something happen in your life that turned you completely away from having faith? Do you have to see in order to believe? Do you believe in God—I mean *really* believe in God? Whom would you affect if you gave up on believing in the notion of having faith?

George Land[1] founded a research and consulting institute to study the enhancement of creative performance. He said, "We are naturally creative and as we grow up we learn to be uncreative." When I read this quote, I thought, *Wow, we are born with an immeasurable amount of faith. I wonder, as we grow and experience life happenings, do we then stop believing in the things that we cannot see?* "Now faith is the substance of things hoped for, the evidence of things not seen." Just have faith!

When I was a little girl, elementary-school age, we went to live with my big mama; it only lasted for maybe a month. I remember praying, crying, and praising the Lord with my big mama. I did not know much about faith, but I believed whatever she believed at the time. Of course, my mom was a believer too; she did not worship like my big mama, but she believed in the gospel. Now that I am older and look back at their situations and how they handled things, I do not believe that either one of those beautiful and intelligent women was walking in the faith and power that God had given them. I love them both, but I wish that they had allowed God to order their steps exceeding abundantly above all that they could have thought or asked. They would have experienced a much richer and more peaceful life. I can honestly say this because I am experiencing a more peaceful life as I grow older.

I did not embrace having faith until I was middle-school age when I had what could have been a catastrophic situation happen to me. I am not sure if any of my family members remember this day, but I do. I will never forget it. It set the tone for a big portion of my life there afterward. My sister and I were at the neighborhood Laundromat because my mom's washing machine had gone out and needed to be fixed. I believe that they were waiting on a part. It was a dreary day. Rain drizzled down from the sky. The neighbors were in their homes. Normally, all the children would be out playing and the adults sitting on the porch, but not this day. Only a few cars drove down our street.

One of my sisters was sitting in the back of the Laundromat in the window. We were waiting for the clothes to finish. All of a sudden, I heard a door slam. Although I was not at the time that familiar with the Holy Spirit, I believe that the Holy Spirit had me hold up my umbrella. As I did, I saw there was a man reaching toward me. I hit that fool with my umbrella more than one time, at the same time screaming for dear life. We ran down the street. My sister made it home before I did, but as I was running, the man pulled up by the curve. I froze in place, and then he looked at me and said, "I am going to get you." Can you imagine a little girl looking into some old man's eyes as he is telling her he is going to get her if it is the last thing that he does? Well, this was one of the scariest times in my life.

This incident tested my belief and my faith in God. For two weeks straight, this man drove past my mom's house, speaking to everyone. I was so scared I would almost crawl underneath my mom. Sometimes

I would run into the house and just pray. I was so scared sometimes I would dream that a gorilla was outside of my window. I do not believe that anyone can imagine what fear is imposed on a child when that child is threatened by an adult. I did not tell my mom, because my mom at the time was a little off the chain. That brother and his entire family would have died. My mom would have killed him and anyone else in her path trying to get to him. I'm so glad that did not have to happen.

I continued to pray about my situation, but one particular day, I prayed a specific prayer. I told God that I was very scared and that I could not take being afraid anymore. I told Him that I did not want to tell my mom about the man who had attempted to rape me or kill me—I am not sure what that man wanted to do to me. I asked God to make him disappear. A couple of days later, he was killed. Now, I was a child, so I started to believe that I had caused his demise. I also became a little afraid of asking for specific things. Nevertheless, I do know that I had no doubt whatsoever in faith. My faith increased tremendously. I knew that I believed in God and in faith. I knew that God would take care of any situation. I am not saying that God killed the man; whatever happened, I believe that he brought it upon himself. Besides, I am just saying he was out of my life. Just have faith!

Although I was a true believer at some point in my young adult life, I began to decrease in the things that were of righteousness and to conform to ungodly situations. The more I became involved in corrupt communication and wickedness, the more I began having to see things before I would believe that things could happen for me. I did not stop praying, and I did not stop believing; I was not disinterested, but that holy thing I had had when I was a little girl was not there anymore. No, He was there, but I was not allowing Him to have His way. I had allowed my worldliness to begin to dictate to me the dos and don'ts of life.

One of the major things that I was not doing as much was reading God's word. "Study to shew thyself approved unto God, a workman that needeth not to be ashamed, rightly dividing the word of truth. But shun profane and vain babblings: for they will increase unto more ungodliness" (2 Timothy 2:15–16). I had stopped reading the Word of God consistently; sometimes I would not take the time to read His word at all. Of course, when I attended church, I would read whatever scripture the pastor requested the congregation to read, but I do not believe that I even bequeathed attention to it. Now I shouted, cried, and felt very good during the service, but I did not do the most important thing, and that is get into His Word and meditate on it. Often, I could not tell you the meaning or title of the sermon.

How can you decipher correct or incorrect information if you do not study? You do know that this is how we pass on profane and vain babbling. Stop the madness, and begin studying God's Word. Study all the topics that interest you, research, read, and listen to many different forms of materials to get an understanding.

Since the beginning of time, we have wavered in our faith. Take for instance Saul. You will find this story in the Bible in 1 Samuel. I am paraphrasing and not giving you the complete story here. What I want you to see is how we need to walk in our faith and trust in God.

Saul was the first king of Israel. Saul was handsome and physically appealing to the eyes, according to the Word. How did he become the first king of Israel? God had delivered Israel out of Egypt from the hand of the Egyptians and from all who had oppressed them. You remember the Red Sea parting? This was part of the deliverance. Although the Israelites had God's favor, they wanted more; they always wanted more. Does this sound familiar to you—always wanting more? Well, God answered their cry to have a human leader. It was crazy. There was absolutely no reason. Yet they did. The King of Kings, Lord of Lords treats you as special, and you have the nerve to ask Him for a king to lead you.

There is another lesson that I learned in this story that is very important, and it is that our God is intentional. Saul was out looking for his father's donkeys, and it seems like that was the only thing on his mind. The prophet Samuel met and anointed Saul as king of Israel. This was God's plan. Have you ever had an experience in life that altered the way you think and live? Saul became the king of Israel, and initially, he was doing a good job at leading the people. At some point, he overstepped his authority. You know some folks do not know how to handle authority.

The Philistines were planning to go into battle with Israel. Saul was given specific instructions to wait for the prophet Samuel for seven days. I am sure that it was regarding the upcoming battle. Seven days passed, so Saul thought that he had to do something. His faith in what he was told about the soon-to-be battle and what he had experienced went right out the door into the universe. He decided to do what he thought was right in his own mind. It cost him a relationship with God, and he eventually lost the title of king of Israel. Read the story; it is interesting. Do you remember hearing about King David? He took Saul's place as king of Israel, appointed by God; he was a man after God's own heart.

We need to be still and listen to the voice of God. Sometimes God speaks to us in different ways, using friends, family, events, pictures, prayer lines, and many other things to help us. Too often, our own experiences and beliefs wrap so tightly around our minds that we cannot hear Him. Take a moment and ask God to create in you a clean heart, and ask Him to give you wisdom in everything you do. Ask Him to increase your faith. Then just have faith that it is well!

At twenty-one, I joined the army and began to travel to many different parts of the world. Oh, I really got beside myself—at least that is what my mom told me. She was right. When I look back on some of the experiences I encountered, I do believe that God blessed me with an immeasurable amount of faith and favor. Nevertheless, before joining the service, I had already begun a life that set me on a path that led me to believe that what I was doing was not pleasing in God's eyes; therefore, I began to feel like a bad girl. Rather than repenting, I began to do more things outside of my character. I started to believe that I was not a part of the holy thing anymore. I am sure that this was a trick of the enemy. Have faith that God loves you no matter what you do or say. You have to repent, and you have to turn your life around.

I was intimate with a young man when I was close to graduating from high school; I truly thought that I was in love with him. However, for some reason, my mind went back to the man who tried to get me when I was a little girl. The act of being with someone felt good in the moment and very dirty after the fact. I did not feel love from a man until two years after I was married to my husband. The more God increases my faith, the more I experience love. If you are having intimate moments with someone who is not your husband or wife, stop. Have faith that the right person will enter your life. If you have not been intimate with anyone, great! Do not engage! Having someone to hold you and go into you who truly loves you and whom you love is the best thrill ever.

Why did I share this with you? Well, when I was acting impure, I was almost afraid to pick the Bible up and read God's Word. I believe a part of me liked some of the things I was doing. I really enjoyed going out to the clubs partying. I loved dancing; I could dance until the club doors closed. Drinking, smoking, and drugging I could do without, but dropping it like it was hot was my thing. There was always a holy thing inside of me, reminding me that I was in the wrong place or doing the wrong thing.

The more I began to conform to things like staying out all night, ignoring the voice of God, going to church whenever I felt like it, and much more, the further away from His Word I became. I thank God that He does not let His children go. In addition, I thank God that my mom and big mama introduced Him to me. I believe that because I was introduced to Him at an early stage in my life, I could never totally let Him go. Introduce your children to God. I know some folks will ask why. My answer would be, "Why not? Everything else is being introduced to them; why not introduce them to righteousness?" Introduce them to the Bible, a manual that will guide them through life. Just have faith!

There is a power in having faith. Think about it. We are born with faith. Sit back and watch a baby. Watch him or her closely because babies do things suddenly. A baby will roll, stick things into his or her little mouth, touch fire, and jump from a bed into your arms. Babies do things in their diapers that are choking, but they trust you to keep them clean. They trust you; this is why they jump without wondering whether you will catch them. They initially touch a hot plate or fire if you do not stop them, because they feel safe in your arms. They feel safe in their surroundings. They do not know the danger that often lurks around them until it is introduced to them. I do not know anyone who remembers events that happened when he or she was a little baby. I guess it is that way for a reason.

If we could hold on to the faith of a baby and have it increase as we grow older, I mean, never being infected, I guess we could blow our breath on a sick person and think healing and that person would be healed from cancer, healed from headaches, healed from all diseases. Where is our faith? I wonder why we conform to worldly things when we know how good it is to have His will on Earth as it is in Heaven.

I wonder why some of us wander in the wilderness of insanity so long before we surrender our lives to God. I am considered a senior citizen in some places, and I spent most of my young adult life ping-ponging back and forward in a world that was not giving me peace. Oh, how I love Jesus because He first loved me. God has increased my faith more than the faith of a mustard seed, and this peace that I have is like the breeze that you feel on a perfect day. It is as a little baby held by his or her parents, feeling safe in their arms.

I regret some of the things that I did in the past, but I also rejoice at the learning experiences because my past is what thrust me into the connection that I have with God, His true word, and that holy thing that dwells inside of me. I was reading one of Smith Wigglesworth's books.[2] In the book, he stated, "Faith laughs at impossibilities and says it will be done." This statement is so profound. Think about it. When you say no, faith says yes. When you cannot see, faith has already seen. When you can no longer push, faith has already pushed it over. When you cannot pay the bills, faith has already cancelled the debt. When you see death, faith sees life. I could go on and on, but you get my point.

I read in one of Smith Wigglesworth's books that human weaknesses could spoil the effectiveness of faith. When I first read this statement, I thought about my past and how I gave in to many temptations that hindered my spiritual growth as well as my progression in life. At some point, I did not believe as I did when I was that little girl on my knees asking God to save me from the bad man. When I prayed that evening, asking God to save me, I had faith that God would handle the situation. Later in life, toxic things had me believing in what I could see. Worldliness increased, and the things of God decreased.

I am so thankful that I am in another place in my life. You can be too. I was reading somewhere that advised not to let the enemy push us in the wrong direction. Well, you do know that in most cases, you are your own worst enemy. Many times, we have more faith in ourselves than we do in God. I still have those moments. I will say that I have faith that God will and impatiently, like Saul, attempt to get the job done in my time and in my will. Although it may seem like all things work out, it never fails that it does not work out effectively. Have faith in God, and watch Him move in your life exceedingly. "Call unto me, and I will answer thee, and shew thee great and mighty things, which thou knowest not" (Jeremiah 33:3). Trust in God and just have faith!

The illustration in this chapter is a visual of how I saw my journey and how I have seen others'. The rope represents faith. We are born with the gift of faith. The baby in the picture holds onto faith without wavering at all. Then as we grow older, it takes a little more to continue to trust the gift of faith. By the time I reached adulthood, my faith was wavering all over the place. I believed, but I was not receiving what I believed and was not totally trusting in God. As an adult, I began to trust people and situations more than I trusted the God who created me and the people I trusted. It took a lot for me to hold on to my faith. I thank God that He placed that rope back in my hands and pulled me out of the darkness. He allowed me to hold on to my faith. We must learn to hold on to our faith. How do we do that? The answer is trust Him! Just have faith.

Chapter 3

MY BUSINESS AND FAITH
(PASSION AND PROFIT)

$\mathcal{D}$o you really want to be an entrepreneur? Do you have a passion for business? Do you love the career that you are pursuing or presently in? Do you like your job? If you are in business, is your business generating you profit? Do you have a specific goal in life? What are you passionate about? Do you only exist? Stop the madness! Just have faith.

Although this chapter is about my journey with business, it is for those of you who are considering entrepreneurship, those who are already in business, and those who do not have a solid direction in life. This chapter is going to seem as though it has nothing to do with the other portions of the book, but let me tell you up front that faith has everything to do with what you pursue in life.

There are so many who go into business without thinking about the real reasons for establishing a business. Some accept jobs to acquire a paycheck; some enter college without a focus. The first time I entered college, I did not pursue my passion and I had no focus. Too often, we do not research or reflect on the business or career that we want to pursue.

Many are in businesses and careers that they do not even like. What a mind- and body-draining experience, spending so much time and energy doing something just because! To clarify this statement, you could truly make a living, even become rich (money), opening a restaurant. People love eating. However, if you do not like to eat, cook, or be around food and people, this business is going to be work for you because it is not your passion. This concept also applies to those of you who are working for someone else.

Passion is a deep, burning love for something or somebody. You just want it and need whatever the thing is, and it makes you happy and joyful. It gives you peace and long-suffering. Yes, if you have true passion for something or somebody, you will definitely experience or be able to identify the fruits of the spirit. Take the time to read Galatians in the Bible; you are going to find the fruits of the spirit in Galatians 5:22–23: "But the fruit of the Spirit is love, joy, peace, longsuffering, gentleness, goodness, faith, meekness, temperance: against such there is no law." You really need to understand what you are passionate about before venturing into entrepreneurship, college, careers, relationships, and work. If you identify your passion and pursue your passion, profit will flow.

Let me identify passion. I am going to give you a simplistic definition and a few examples of passion. I believe that passion is a feeling that never escapes the margins of your mind. Passion never escapes the heart's desires or the soul's longings. It is loving something so deeply that your heart cannot release it, no matter what twists and turns life brings. Passion is like a husband holding you early in the morning, and when the alarm goes off and you have to get up and get ready for work, you wish that you could stop time so that he could continue to hold you. Passion is what Christ had for me and for you when He went to the cross for us. He loved us that much. Whatever you choose to do in life, love it!

When I was a little girl, I used to draw sketches of clothing, hats, shoes, and folks dancing, and I would sit and think about events. I would watch cartoons, *American Bandstand*, and *Soul Train* and wonder how they put those shows together. I would smile when I would see an outstanding outfit or a scene with an incredible background. I would sit and dream about traveling all over the world. My mom always had a beautiful picture hanging somewhere on the wall, and I would sit and look at those pictures and take myself inside that scene. I remember experiencing such joy when my mind returned from the land of imagination.

The black-and-white classics on television were my favorites because of the actors' charm, beauty, and poise. My mother was classic with a hint of a gun-slinging mentality. I loved all of it. I would dream of a huge blue wave on which I would dance and sometimes model; I never saw where the wave and activities would end, but the scene would bring me so much joy and excitement. Embracing those moments of imagination took me away from the ordinary events of my childhood.

When I entered elementary school, I had a blast. I remember the plays and singing in the choir was so much fun for me. I can still remember playing a role in *Jack and the Beanstalk* and helping to make the arrangements. Then I remember singing in a show with my friends. I was a backup singer for my girlfriend. She could really sing; I could only perform. We sang "Mr. Big Stuff," and boy did we have fun! We brought down the little house too. It did not stop in elementary school. I went on to middle school and then high school, and my first major event was in the news; it was a fashion show, and I was one of the directors.

Later I joined the drama club in high school. By the end of my high school years, I was not too happy about how things were going. In my tenth-grade year, we were bused to a school across town. Everything I was passionate about began to sink in quicksand. Then I joined the debate club. I joined the debate club out of anger, not passion. These events happened so many years ago, but I still remember the passion and some of the pain. I still have these memories as though they happened yesterday.

Passion is not something that you find at the bottom of quicksand, because it will rise repeatedly. We suppress it, but what we are passionate about will remain in our spirit. This is why it is so important that you identify what you are passionate about and pursue the passion. It will bring you the fruits of the spirit; it will bring you profit. Parents, help your children identify their passions and support their passions, even if what they seem to embrace does not look like a money-maker. We have the tendency to influence others to do what we think is best for them. Some of you influence others to move toward your passions—you know what I mean.

By the time I reached the tenth grade, I knew what I wanted to do. My drama teacher had even expressed to me that I should pursue a career in acting or directing; the world of legitimate entertainment, which I thought was my imagination, was my passion. But I couldn't see myself making a profit being an event planner, choreographer, director, or fashion designer. These things were my passion, but I had not identified them as being a passion and surely had not embraced them as being a nourishing lifestyle; therefore, my energies went toward pieces of my passion and pieces of my whatever. I went to college to be an administrative assistant; they said there would be money in it. Nevertheless, I never lost my passion for the scenes that played out in my head.

One night, I was listening to the radio, and an army commercial came on. It talked about traveling around the world. I had to see Paris (arts, clothes, and beautiful sceneries) and Washington DC (money, power, and the president of the United States of America), and I wanted the experiences passionately. I joined the military and traveled to those places and others. While I was in the military, my passions continued to surface. With others, I volunteered to help organize fashion shows, parades, talent shows, and other events.

I was a material supply specialist. It served me well, but it was not my passion. Eventually, I met the most wonderful man in the world, my husband, Theodore E. Minnitt Jr., an Alabama jewel. We married and had a beautiful baby boy, Terrance Y. Minnitt. We continued to travel with the military. At some point, I lost sight of my directions and passion. I begin to immerse myself into what made immediate profit. It did not have to be a part of my passion. We do this thing when profit and confusion exceed passion.

When you do not follow your passion, confusion sets in, and then your whatevers become your life, leaving you either wondering why you feel the way you do about your life or finding yourself in rabbit mode, hopping from job to job, place to place, and person to person. What is terrible is when you find yourself in Dead Sea mode. This is when your life stops flowing. It feels like the currents in your life no longer flow and everything seems to die or just stand still. Identify your passions, and embrace, love, and pursue them. Have faith in the thing that the Holy Spirit places in your spirit to do.

Commit to what you are passionate about immediately with urgency, whether it is on a job or as an entrepreneur. Understand that passion is passion whether you are sharing your passion on a job or in your own business. Whatever you do, do not open a business solely based on making a profit. Do not pursue a career solely based on making a profit. Your passion will bring you profit. "Hope deferred maketh the heart sick; but when the desire cometh, it is a tree of life" (Proverbs 13:12).

Parents, teachers, guardians, uncles, aunts, and other stakeholders in the lives of children, observe the children that you are privileged to encounter and notice the activities in their lives that bring joy to them, the things that excite them the most, and their passions, and expose them to more of their passions. If you are unable to expose them, get books and talk about the things that they are passionate about. Not all children are self-motivated, and some are unable to identify the things that they love the most. Do not be so quick to push children into college without knowing their passion. Their passions will help them to determine their life direction. We do not want our children to enter into a Dead Sea mode.

You do not have to be an entrepreneur to be happy, but you must be embracing your passion to acquire true happiness. I hope that up until this point you at least have thought about your passion or passions. Now ask yourself, "Am I in a job or career that is a part of my passion?" or "Am I the owner of a business that is a part of my passion?" Also ask, "Am I enjoying the fruits of the spirit, or am I just working it out day by day just because?" "Better is a little with righteousness than great revenues without right" (Proverbs 16:8). It cannot be a good thing to live life without a purpose. Without passion, your purpose is hoodwinked; get out of the rabbit or Dead Sea mode, find your passion, and embrace it. As one of the great bishops of all time, Bishop T. D. Jakes,[1] says, "Live on purpose!" Bishop Jakes has a DVD series on this topic and workbooks to study with the DVD. It is an awesome series.

I say, "Live life every day with the end in mind. Live every day passionately!" My personal motto for life is "Love hard, work hard, and play hard!" For the children of the world, observe them, allow them to find their passion, and then let them embrace it, even if it is cleaning toilets. Passion will bring them profit.

Let me give you a simplistic definition and a few examples of profit. I am a certified business composite retired teacher/administrator who believes that profit is what you gain from selling an object, place, or thing. For example, say you purchase a dress, shoes, and jewelry from a clothing retail business and your bill totals $1,250.46 plus tax. The clothing retail business made a *profit* from the sale of the items. I wear wigs and hair extensions all the time. In addition, I enjoy the pampering of a good manicure and pedicure with a hot towel laid on my neck; this costs money. We have to pay for the extra hair and the manicure and pedicure services; the salon makes a profit for rendering their services. The beauty supply stores make a profit for providing us with our extra hair. I like to believe that we raised our son to be a caring and loyal person; our hearts profit from the things that he has shown us throughout his life.

Profit is a gain and benefit in the form of currency and other returns and benefits. Many people focus on the currency part of profit and forget that profit means more than just acquiring money. I had a conversation with someone near and dear to me about profit; he had not thought about profit other than in the form of money. I said to him, "You know, profit is more than just having cash." He said it was about money, so I paraphrased Mark 8:36: "For what shall it profit a man, if he shall gain the whole world, and lose his own soul." He said, "That is a biblical term. We are talking about business." Think about this scripture.

When thinking about profit, often we do not think about it in the sense of gaining or losing something; like my dear friend, we only think of profit in the form of money. Profit is so much bigger than the dollar bill. If we thought of profit differently, many households, businesses, cities, and nations would be better off. The next time you receive a sum of money, stop before you spend it and ask yourself if what you are spending it on will benefit you. In addition, if you are the head of an organization and have influence on how the funding received is spent in that organization, ask if the organization will benefit from how funds are spent. However you spend money in your household or in a business, it will affect everything and everybody associated with the decision in a positive or negative way.

When people allow profit to be the driving force in their lives, they begin to do things without a conscience, like selling drugs that kill or alter the minds of others; some drug dealers make a lot of money but contribute to harming many lives. Families separate daily because they lose sight of what matters the most in their relationships. Too often, they gain currency, and the currency becomes more important than gains in the form of love. If families would take the time to embrace a passion for their families, then money would not be able to divide them.

Now some of you are probably wondering, *What does this have to do with deciding whether you want to be an entrepreneur?* Passion is equal to profit, and profit is more than gaining money. Part of deciding if you want to be an entrepreneur is deciding what your passion is and then determining your mind-set regarding profit. In addition, do you have faith in your decisions?

I have worked many jobs and owned a few businesses; in my latter years, I discovered that many of the jobs that I worked I worked for money; I needed the money to get the things that I wanted and a few things that I actually needed. I did not think about what I was gaining for my mind, body, soul, and others. I was just thinking about making some money to get more stuff. It never occurred to me that if I had followed my passions, I would not have wasted time on so many different things that did not soothe my spirit or soul at all. Many leaders, when making decisions for organizations, cities, and even nations, think first of the money. Sometimes, they give no thought to how the spending of the money will affect the whole. We really need to change how we view profit.

Righteous passion will bring you righteous profit! Identify what you are passionate about, and then identify what profit really means to you. Once you develop an understanding of these two words, ask yourself what it is you are truly passionate about and begin to position yourself to gain profit.

Three years ago, I worked out at a gym located in Killeen, Texas. Every day they would place a quote on their blackboard. One particular quote hit me like a quarterback throwing fifteen balls into my chest at 190 miles per hour. It stated, "So many people spend their health gaining wealth and then have to spend their wealth regaining back their health." This is why it is so very important that you are living your life on purpose and in line with your spirit, body, and soul. It will profit you in the long run. What are you profiting from what you are doing? Passion equals profit! Do you have faith in your answer?

On the following lines, write down one thing or more that you are passionate about.

_____

_____

_____

_____

_____

_____

Think about it! Now on the following lines, in one paragraph, identify how your passion has brought you profit or how your passion can help you profit (remember profit goes beyond money). Do you have faith in your answer?

_____

_____

_____

_____

_____

_____

_____

_____

_____

Stop using your passion as just a hobby; it is a gift from God Almighty, a very special gift. Use it to help build your dreams, so that you are able to help others build theirs. I have seen so many people with extraordinary talents. I recall a young woman working as a school aide, and for school events, she created websites and posters that generally you would have to pay major money to have created. When we asked, "Why are you not doing this for pay?" Her answer was: "Oh, I just do this for fun. I love doing this." I just wanted to scream, "Stop it! Just stop it! Live your life on purpose!" Passion and profit move the earth in a righteous or unrighteous way, whether you are an entrepreneur or whether you work for a company.

Are you using your passion as just a hobby? Yes _____ No _____

Are you using your passion to build profit for yourself, your family, your friends, your seeds and future seeds, your city, your country, or God's kingdom on earth? Yes _____ No _____

If you checked no for either one of these questions, stop reading for a moment and go back to the drawing board. Assess your passion again, and determine how you may use your passion for someone other than yourself. If you work for a company, that company should stand for something; you are a part of what it stands for. If you decide to become an entrepreneur, your company should stand for something. "A man's gift maketh room for him, and bringeth him before great men" (Proverbs 18:16). You know that you are great! Have faith in the things God has granted to you.

The last business I opened before writing this book was called Fan Minnitt Arts, Gifts, and Fashion. I believed that the Holy Spirit quickened my spirit to open this business just as I believe that the Holy Spirit hastened my spirit to write this book. The difference in my belief now versus then is that I received what I believed and my faith is stronger than ever. God made provisions for me to take my business around the world; my faith wavered, and I started to look for things to happen versus allowing God to happen. I could not decrease self; therefore, I was not allowing the Holy Spirit to increase in the business. I closed the business December 2010.

We were featured in the local newspaper three times; we were also featured in a local magazine. God afforded us the luxury of running a television commercial for one year. A prophet stopped me outside of the store one day and prophesied to me that my business would be very successful and that it would be known all over the world. With all mentioned, because I could not see it profiting (money), I was not willing to endure, and I have to admit my faith decreased, my belief decreased, and my trust in God wavered. I learned many lessons from that business experience. The best lesson I learned from Fan Minnitt Arts, Gifts, and Fashion is faith is the substance of things hoped for and the evidence of things not seen. Trust in God, and stop looking for things from your own point of view. Ask Him for wisdom and knowledge and to order every step you take in life. Walk in it, my sisters and brothers! Walk in it! Then just have faith!

Chapter 4

MY MOM AND FAITH (DEMENTIA/ALZHEIMER'S)

Have you ever lost a loved one to a dreadful disease? Have you encountered a sudden change in a loved one's behavior that confused you? Have you ever questioned God with a why? Have you ever been angry with yourself because you just did not know what to do? We know that everybody has to die one day, so why is it so hard when death visits one of our family members' or friends' lives?

This chapter was one of the hardest chapters for me to write and will probably be the hardest chapter in this book for you to read. It started out being about me. Nevertheless, after giving it some thought, I wrote it for me and for you. I wrote for me because I believe I need to get it out of my emotions. I am writing for you because I feel there is someone who is reading this book who needs healing and peace of mind from what he or she is experiencing or from what he or she has already experienced. Know that it is going to be all right with you if you have faith that you have no control over the situation you are encountering or the situation that you faced. The battle is not yours; it is the Lord's. Trust God! Have faith that He can and He will!

Dementia is a dreadful disease that no one should ever have to live through or witness. Though no disease is welcomed, nevertheless, this one is like watching a person die a slow death by torture. On April 26, 2012, my mom passed away in a nursing home early in the morning. They wrote down that she died from natural causes. For the life of me, I am not sure why they called seven years of Alzheimer's and eventually a type of leukemia natural.

I had taken off from work that morning to visit with my mom the entire day. When I walked into her room, she was sitting straight up with her eyes wide open and a river of white foam rushing out of her mouth like a flash flood. She was dying. The nurses and staff thought that they had revived her. I did not; I saw death. I did not stay in the room. I watched her sleeping, and she looked like she was resting. Call me whatever, but that was the first time in a long time she looked at peace. I did not want to see her take her last breath. I did not want to hold her either. It was as if time had stopped.

Suddenly, the nurse came out of her room, crying, and told me, "I am sorry. She is gone."

"She is gone!" I was already mourning, but I had to pull myself together and call my family. It is crazy how you think in times like this. I sat down across from the bed that my mama lay in dead. I could hear her saying, "You'd better not let folks see my hair like this." So I called my friend who is a master cosmetologist in Copperas Cove. She was my mama's hair stylist. She was the first to hear that Mama was gone. Her shop was near the nursing home, and she said, "Girl, I'll be there." Then I began to call my family. Later, my son arrived, and we sat and just stared.

I am not a doctor. I had to research dementia and Alzheimer's after the doctor told me that my mom had dementia. I was very confused initially. I read about it and asked a million questions. When someone diagnoses you or a loved one with an illness, please ask questions; it will help you to move through the process with a little more dignity and understanding.

Under the title of *dementia*, there are different types, which are characterized by abnormal neurodegeneration.[1] My mother was diagnosed with Alzheimer's disease. Alzheimer's causes a loss of memory and the ability to think clearly.

My mother endured a horrible experience before we brought her to the town where my family resided. A transient from the state of Louisiana who was a victim of the Katrina hurricane had taken over her life. He took her medicine, money, ID—everything but her physical life. Could we have avoided this? Yes!

During the month of July, Mom and I went to the casino for her birthday. She loved the casino, and she won sometimes. I did a lot of looking and eating. I knew not to bother her when she was pulling the handle of the slot machine. After that weekend, I called, and she told me that her phone was messing up and needed repairs. She did not have a cell phone because one had been stolen and another lost; she could not do the cell phone thing.

I told her I would return in August, after the first week of school and I was going to have some crazy stories to share. I suggested maybe we would take another trip. So I continued with my busy life, and two months passed. Then a call from my cousin came; he said, "Fertitta, you'd better come check on your mom. Something is not right." I told my husband that I had to go home and check on Mom. I took off from work and asked my cousin to meet me in my hometown at three in the afternoon. I praise God that he decided to go to Mom's earlier. There was a victim of Hurricane Katrina there. He should have been in a mental institution. He was free because records were not available. He had taken over my mother's life.

When my cousin arrived, he had to threaten to call the police because whatever my mom did that day, someone called the number for neglected seniors. I am so grateful for whoever made that call. They were going to have her admitted to a state hospital. She was in bad shape, and the transient was trying to make decisions for her. My cousin took the keys from the transient and told the senior care representative that she had a daughter who was on her way and that I was five hours away. I never thought about this, but what was the likelihood of my cousin, who does not live in my hometown, calling that day? God is good. God protected her even under the circumstances. He did not allow the devil to take her life or for her to be raped or beaten or suffer continued abuse. My cousin asked that they wait and to give me an opportunity to make it home and help make decisions for my mom. She remembered my cousin but was still afraid to talk.

When I arrived and saw my mom, instantly, my soul crumpled. Nevertheless, I had to remember that God is real, what was happening was real, and that I had to be strong and trust in the Lord to give me strength and wisdom and to increase my faith. I also needed Him to keep me from evil. It would not grieve me. If that man would have shown up again at the time when we were trying to see what was going on, I think I would have attempted murder in the first degree. When my mom saw me, she called my nickname and seemed to be comforted. I was able to get things rolling on her behalf. To this day, I believe that my mom had a nervous breakdown, which caused the final onset of dementia. People, do not take your loved ones for granted. Being busy can never take the place of love lost.

My mom was admitted to the hospital for evaluation, and this is when we received the news that she had dementia and other issues. I did not accept the diagnosis in my heart or mind. I believed that once she was stabilized with her medication, we went shopping for a pretty outfit, and she sprayed a little Chanel or White Diamond on, she would be just fine, and then we could go back and begin to deal with whatever we had to. Everything would be all right.

It was not until years later that I accepted what was going on with my mama. I was in denial from the beginning while I was going through fighting to keep her away from what she could no longer call home and fighting for her life, a life that would never be the same, and fighting for my life, which internally, twisted up in knots. I blamed myself for everything that had happened.

I knew something was not right that July. Her makeup was not appropriately applied. I did not think that she was forgetful, but she was paranoid and would not let me take care of any of her business. This was before July. Although I am married with a child, I did not know how to battle with my mom. She was Mama. She was Big Mama. She was the strongest woman in the world that I knew. God trusted her to raise me, and she did a good job. Therefore, I believe, over time, it was easier for me to ignore the fact that something was truly going wrong in my mother's life. Do not ignore the signs you see and hear. Do not be afraid to go into battle with a loved one. Research, and make some calls for help! Whatever you do, *do not* allow denial to enter into your being and do not turn away or procrastinate. Just have faith and fight!

One day while sitting in the nursing home listening to my mama playing the piano, I asked myself, *Why did you not go back in August when in fact you knew something was not right? Was it because she would never allow you to follow through whenever you started to help? Was it because you really did not know what to do or what you were dealing with? Was it because it was destroying you inside and it became a matter of self-survival?* I have always had a creative imagination. I pretended at different times that everything was all right. However, that day, listening to her play "Lean on Me" on the piano, the answer became very clear to me: I needed help myself.

Knowing that people are being educated on Alzheimer's was a godsend. There were so many things that my family faced because of ignorance of what we were experiencing with this disease. Looking back, in hindsight, I can see that my mother needed help long before the day my cousin called.

What do you pray for when your mother is in trouble and you become frightened out of your good senses? The saddest part about this entire ordeal is that I did not realize that I was not truly trusting in God to handle things, so I began to fall mentally weak. If you try to act or think in a weak state of mind, it may or may not work. You have to have faith that God, the creator of all things, can and will allow things to happen in life.

We often question some of the things He allows to happen; I did. Do not feel guilty about asking God questions. He is a good God, and He understands our mind, body, soul, and spirit. He knows our level of faith, pain, wisdom, and strength. His word says in Romans 8:28: "And we know that all things work together for good to them that love God, to them who are the called according to his purpose." This scripture and prayer helped me so many times during this process. I asked God, and I still do, to increase my faith. This helped me to get through the worst parts of Mom's condition and trials. I asked God for wisdom and knowledge about Alzheimer's, and I believe that He answered my prayers and helped me to find the answers that I needed in order to understand how to help my mom.

There was a time when the nursing home wanted to evict my mom for her behavior. I frequented this place, signing in most of the time, but the way I found out about the eviction was by mail. It would not have been so depleting had they called me into the office and had a conversation with me. This letter brought me to my knees; it brought me right back into the past. Old feelings and fears resurfaced. I told my mom that I would never let anyone hurt her again and that I would be there for her.

Although I am a praying woman, I felt like my soul was smothering. I called a friend who is a prayer warrior and a very smart woman, crying about my situation. She told me to contact an organization that helped with senior citizens and other matters. Knowledge is power, wisdom is a golden key, and having faith in it all will keep you standing strong, even when you are weak. This organization helped to reverse the eviction and to give the nursing home some valuable feedback. Training with patients like my mom was implemented in their establishment, and my mom's behavior was stabilized until her death. It was not perfect, but things got much better. My family and I were able to enjoy quality time with Mom.

In February 2012, once again, they admitted my mom to the hospital. This was not the first time. Nevertheless, when they called me this time, they were not asking me if I wanted to come and follow the ambulance;

she was already en route. This was not a good sign. They communicated with me on everything and would always give me an opportunity to get to my mom before placing her in an ambulance.

This particular day, I called my friend, Vi, who had been shopping with Mama and me on occasions. I asked her to meet me at the hospital. I felt like this was not going to turn out right for some reason. The doctor spoke with me, and he told me that they had found why my mom was losing blood (they never could tell where the blood was going); they just knew she was losing it. He told me, and I guess the nurse saw the blank look on my face. I did not understand the doctor. She finally broke it down for me. My mom had a type of leukemia. I looked at my friend with tears in my eyes. Neither one of us said a word. I knew that evening that my mama would never enter another hospital.

Before the doctor and nurse gave me the information, Mama and I were watching television and she was talking. For one instant, she stopped rambling, looked at me, and was in her right mind; she even looked like her normal self. She said, "Titta, I am tired of this. I am tired, baby." For the first time, my heart was ready to release.

You see, a year before this date, something similar had happened. They immediately had to rush Mama to the hospital. I had had the same feeling. But all the way to the hospital, I prayed to God, asking Him to take care of my mom, and I started saying out loud, "Mama, don't do this to me, not now. I really can't take you leaving me right now. You know how I am. Do not do this now." I told God, "You said You would not give us more than we could bear. I really cannot endure this right now." (I was convinced at the time that what I had stated was biblical.) I can image God saying, "I did not tell her that." He probably told the angels, "Go down and help my child because this burden is more than she can handle."

Back to the hospital room in February 2012—I looked at her and said, "Mama, do what you have to do. I love you." She went back into that confused state. I went back into my norm, and all was well until April 26, 2012 (two months later), around ten o'clock in the morning.

The lesson I learned from this seven-year battle with Alzheimer's was: you won't always be able to fix things, no matter how much you want to; nevertheless, trust God and just have faith!

The illustration in this chapter is a reminder of how God has always taken care of us. He led the Israelites with clouds by day and fire by night. When Moses and the children of Israel came to a dead end at the Red Sea—"Oh, how great a thing"—God allowed Moses to divide the Red Sea, and he and the people walked the path to the other side. They were free from Pharaoh's army. Pharaoh's army drowned moving through that same path.

In August 2014, I had an opportunity to walk on the bottom of the ocean in Punta Cana, Dominican Republic. I will remember this experience for the rest of my life. There was so much water all around and over us. Of course, we had the proper breathing equipment and divers to ensure that we did not have a moment under the water. When I think about all that water, I cannot imagine walking and seeing a huge wall of water on each side of me with no glass, no breathing equipment, and no divers suited up. It brings tears to my eyes.

The Israelites had one thing, and that was faith in the God who ordered their steps. Stop for one minute or more, and ask God to order your every step and to increase your faith. In addition, praise Him as long as you want to. Praise His holy name! Praise Him for all the Red Seas that He has parted for you. Praise Him for all the times He did not allow Pharaoh to destroy you. Praise Him; trust Him. Just have faith!

The woman you see getting out of the hospital bed in the illustration represents a call to action; God never stops leading us by day or night. He never stops making a way out of no way. Rise, rise, and take back what the enemy has taken from you. Rise, and take back your mind, health, finances, children, families, wealth, beliefs, and righteous thinking. Take it back. Get up!

Despite the Alzheimer's, He took care of my mom. He took care of my family. God was always there for us. I know that He was, or I would have lost my mind. He is always there to help you rise. Just have faith!

Chapter 5

MY JOB AND FAITH (THE MOVE)

"Now faith is the substance of things hoped for and the evidence of things not seen" (Hebrews 11:1). Many times, I have read Genesis, and the story of Abraham always seems to fascinate me. God told Abraham to get out of his country, away from his father's house, to a land that He would show him. Abraham was seventy-five years old at the time of this command. According to the Word, God told Abraham that He would make him a great nation, bless him, and make his name great. He also told Abraham that he would be a blessing; He would bless those who blessed Abraham and would curse those who cursed him. God said in Abraham all the families of the earth would be blessed. You can find this part of the story in Genesis 12.

Abraham's faith in God was incredible, absolutely off the Richter scale; he was an amazing man of God. He listened to God, trusted God, and moved in the will of God. Did you know that he took his son Isaac to be sacrificed? Remember Isaac was the son that he had with Sarah at an old age. God tested Abraham. Of course, our God is a provider. When Abraham raised his knife to kill Isaac, an angel of the Lord called to him from heaven and said, "Abraham, Abraham! Do not lay your hand on the lad, or do anything to him; for now I know that you fear God, since you have not withheld your son, your only son, from Me." There was a ram caught in a thicket by its horns. Abraham sacrificed the ram. God will always have a ram in the thicket for you. Believe and trust in Him. Read Genesis 22:2–19 for the all-inclusive story. I am telling you the Bible is so enlightening as well as interesting.

What if the Holy Spirit quickens your spirit to do something and you do not hear the reason why? What if your life is peaceful, in order, with no problems, and the Holy Spirit tells you to get out of the town that you live in, to start a new life, and you happen to be in your fifties? Your home is exactly the way you want it, your yard is finally looking good, and you have plans and money for additional home improvements, but you believe that God Himself is directing you to move.

What do you do? Debt is no longer a thought, because your family finally has a handle on that terrible sin. You know that moving is an expense. You have friends you met at the gym and at the restaurant that you eat at at least twice a month; friends you see at professional development meetings, and friends who come over for the holidays and overeat and play games. And you have a son, your only son, who owns his own home and is settled, with no intentions of moving. Additionally, you are making over sixty thousand dollars a year and your husband over ninety-five thousand a year. It is just the two of you, and you do not have to provide for the one son, so you are living pretty well. Your credit allows you to get whatever you want. I had one bad thing on my credit (I thought I had paid my business taxes, but I thought wrong). Fortunately, it did not affect us. What do you do when the stuff opposes the command the Almighty has given? Just have faith!

Let us pause here. Give God the praise, and ask Him to increase your faith. Put the book down if you can, and praise His Holy name! If you are not a believer and you are reading this book, say, just because, ask God for understanding of His word. He will give you the desires of your heart. However, there are things you must do.

Okay, back to what I am writing about in this chapter. My move is a fraction of the task that Abraham had, but I found some similarities and it allowed me to understand what was happening to me and how some things are a move of God and not my own. I knew my destination, and I thought that I knew my purpose. I even thought that it would be a piece of cake moving into my same position. I had checked the salary ranges. I would even have been making a little bit more. True believers know deep down inside that God will provide for them. Therefore, I believed that we would make a move, and everything would be the same, only in another place with different folks.

People, with all that said, my faith wavered. Yes, it did, again. I sure hope that in my latter days, I will stop doubting what I know to be true from God! I was an assistant principal in a district located in Texas. I had taught business for three years and was an assistant principal for nine years. I was also running a business, and taking theology classes at a church in Dallas. During this time, I became addicted to God's word. My drive to classes was two hours and approximately thirty minutes one way on Mondays and Wednesdays or Tuesdays and Thursdays. I was blessed with principals who allowed me to leave at a reasonable time on those days that I had classes and assistant principals who would work with me regarding assistant principal duties. They knew that the drive would be long and that I had to be back at work the next morning. You know, our God is so awesome.

During the time that I was making this five-and-a-half-hour drive, it was not a thought; I probably would have quit if it had been. People would say, "You drive that far after work?" My thought would be, *That is not that far. What's the big deal?* You see, I was not calculating the round-trip. I always had the one-way trip in my mind. Now that I look back on it, I call it a supernatural thing. Forty-five minutes is a big deal to me now! I was seeking God's word. The trip was worth it. If you do not read the Bible, start doing so. Oh, the stories are so intriguing and applicable to everyday living. The Bible is truly a manual for life. Yes, it is!

In addition to the drive to classes, I had to deal with the situation with my mom. You read the story in chapter 4. This added more hours to my driving equation and time working; it was sometimes very stressful. I continued to handle my job, my business, and my family with the grace of our Lord Jesus Christ. I wish that I could mention the school's name and the names of the staff; they were wonderful, and they helped me through the process. God had me in the right place.

I stayed on my job for several years, and I'm not sure if it was day or night or if I was awake or asleep, but it was very clear to me that I had to move to Dallas, Texas. Have you had the urge to do something that you knew would disrupt your life? If so, what did you do? Are you still wondering what to do? It took me a year to finally just have faith.

When I first heard the call to move, my brain cells started to dance around inside of my head. My first thought was, *Is this real? Where is this coming from?* I asked, "God, is this thought coming from you, or is it coming from me?" Eventually, I accepted the fact that the Holy Spirit was responsible for my call to Dallas. I informed my husband, son, and prayer partner, Diane Easter, but I did not tell others until later. I began to remove things out of my office until my office was empty, with the exception of a flower in a vase on my desk and a few other small sculptures and books.

Nevertheless, we did not move that year; my husband was not totally in agreement with moving the first time I made the statement. Furthermore, I did not quite explain to him that the Holy Spirit had told me that we had to move. I am not sure how he would have reacted at that time. Sometimes folks think that you have flown over the cuckoo nest when you say certain things. Some of you reading this book know what I mean.

At the end of that year, there were job openings for a principal at three different campuses. I applied and made the cut for an interview. Now my brain cells began to dance again, but this time my thoughts started spinning like the sun spinning in place waiting for earth's twenty-four-hour rotation. Questions needed answers; I asked myself so many questions. This was a struggle.

This is how it rambled in my thoughts—faith versus flesh, hope versus despair, cannot see versus what I needed to see, just having faith versus wavering. Yep, there was a spiritual battle going on in my mind.

We need a more intimate relationship with God so that the struggle that happens in the mind does not take you over. You have control over what you think and how you process the things that you allow to enter into your mind. Feed your mind with things that create in you a clean heart and right thinking. It is important what you feed your mind. Your life outcomes come from what you think. If you feed your mind with corrupt communication, you get corrupt thinking, which in most cases leads to disorder in your life.

The first question that I asked myself was, "What are you going to do if you are hired?" and then I asked, "What about having faith in a command that you believe came from God?" I must admit again that at the time I was wrestling with the decision to move into another territory. This journey was truly a test of my faith. My belief system was wavering like a confused cockroach sprayed by Raid. Thank God, I was not moved to the second level of the interview process, and I said that because I pray to God to close doors I should not enter and open those that I should enter. That door closed, so I knew I was not to enter it. I knew that I was violating the heavens just by going on the interview. I knew my assignment, and that assignment was to move.

I returned to work the next school term, but this time my faith had increased. Finally, I had placed total trust in God. I informed my husband that we were moving and that we had to. He stated to me, "If you find a job, we will move." I was so happy. The conversation that I had with God was about how my husband did not want to move, and I knew He was not into breaking up marriages. He puts them together. I knew that the Holy Spirit had touched my husband's heart. It was too easy, or so I thought. Getting a job would be a piece of cake. Given all the years of experience that I had with the same district, surely I would be the prime pick of the candidates. We were on our way.

When I returned to work this time, I moved everything out of the office except for the necessities. In addition, I began to take the paintings off the wall at our home; I was packing for the move. I began to put in applications in the area we planned on moving to.

I think I might have put in for a principal/assistant principal position at a hundred or more schools, but I did not get one interview. By this time, I trusted God, and my thought was on moving. I knew that God would provide. I was steadily packing, and my house was a mess. I had no job offers and a husband who, at the time, insisted that I find a job before he would agree to uproot our life.

There was a house for sale on the Internet, which I absolutely fell in love with. Each piece of our furniture had a place in this home. For a year and a half, this house was on the market. This was our home; I knew it was.

Prayer works, and our God will always provide a ram in the thicket. The time came for contract renewal, and I still did not have a job interview or offer in the city we were to move to. Yours truly just had faith that everything was going to take place as the Holy Spirit had placed in my spirit. I even began to see visions of the city outline in my mind. I would get on the Internet and pull up my future home. I would watch it go on and off contract. Some people probably thought at the time that I was a little touched—and not by an angel either.

My supervisor brought me my 2013/14 contract to sign for the following school year; I told her that I was not going to sign the contract because I was not returning the following year. She gave me some good advice, as any supervisor would, and that was, "You do not have a job yet, so sign it." Well, I knew I did not need to sign the contract, because God had my back at this time. After a brief conversation, she told me to sign the contract just in case. I started to sign, knowing I was going to follow the will of the Lord. Then suddenly sentences began to run on pretty ribbons in my mind. "Just in case you do not find a job, sign it." "Just in case you do not move, sign it." "Just in case it takes you a little longer to find a job, sign it." "Just in case you can't trust Me, sign it." I flinched and placed the pen on the desk. I never did finish signing a contract that would have guaranteed employment for the following school year.

I continued to apply for jobs in the territory we had agreed to move into, and after a while I even began to apply outside of that territory. The few friends that I had in the area were giving my name to their friends. Nothing worked. I would always pray to God to close those doors that I should not go through and open those that I should, so when doors were not opening for me, I continued to trust God. Now, was I feeling a little funny after not receiving even one interview out of all the school districts that I had applied to? Who would not? Since I was packing things at home, my husband had begun to ask me, "Have you found a job yet?"

The 2013/14 school year had begun. Now everybody was asking me, "What are you doing? Have you found a job? What is going on?" To be honest, I did not know myself. I just knew that all the doors had closed for me regarding employment in the place where we were to reside. To add to this equation, the home that I had claimed came off the listing. It was under contract once again.

After having a conversation with my husband one day, I decided to apply to be a substitute teacher. He had told me if I got a job, we would move. I am sure that he was talking about getting a job as an administrator. Therefore, I was taking a chance with the substitute teacher thing. I am not sure why, but I did. I was hired, and my husband said, "Okay, we will move." He rented me a hotel in Rockwall for the month of November, and I drove all over Dallas, Fort Worth, and other places that I was not familiar with substitute teaching.

We found a realtor, and he showed me some houses, but for some reason, I could not get the house that I had claimed out of my mind. We were standing in a home that he had shown me; although it was beautiful, I could not get my mind off my home. I asked him to find out if our house was on the market again. He did, and it was. We purchased the house and moved into it December 18, 2013.

The first couple who viewed our previous home purchased it. They wanted our former home as soon as they saw it. At least this is the story we were told. The closing with both homes worked out. Do you know that God gave us double what we had with less money? You see, my husband had to leave his job also, and for the first few months, he was unemployed. He is a retired soldier, so we did have income coming in, but we had taken a major cut in both of our incomes. It did not matter. God provided once again. He will always leave us a ram in the thicket. He is our Jehovah-Jireh (the Lord Will Provide). Just have faith!

The illustration for this chapter is a picture of the contract, which I signed with two letters of my name and stopped. I was not going to break a covenant with God. I had allowed my faith to waver too many times before; it was not going to happen again.

I am issuing a call to action. Whenever God calls you to change and you know that it is God and not yourself, dismiss "just in case." Do not let another "just in case" keep you from your destiny.

JoB
CONTRACT

Sign Just in Case

Faith wavers
Faith wavers

Chapter 6

FAMILY AND FAITH
(STOP THE MADNESS)

*H*ave you spoken to your immediate family lately? Do you use texting, tweeting, and Facebook as your only means of communicating with loved ones? Are you still holding on to anger for someone because he or she owes you money or said something you did not like months or years ago? Do you even know who your extended family is other than the ones you have grown up with in your home? Are you still angry with your mother, father, sister, cousin, or brother for whatever? Do you allow sin to enter into your home willingly? Do you get along with your coworkers? Do you have friends? Do you like yourself?

The answer to many of these questions is pure madness. In order for us to get back on track in this world, we must stop the madness and begin to trust in God! Just have faith!

Generations are broken, unsettled, and lost because of family matters stemming from years of distrust, disbelief, corrupt communication, and conditional love. Isn't this the same with how we treat our God? We trust Him for some things but not with all things. We might believe what we speak, or we might not, and for some reason, we saturate our minds and bodies with corrupt communication. Yes, often we love Him with conditions. We treat God as if He is a secret Santa; as long as the gifts are rolling in, we are happy, but when they stop coming, the thrill flies out the window.

Unfortunately, some of you treat your family members, friends, former friends, and foes the same way. I have been guilty a time or two myself. I have done some extensive traveling in my life and have met many folks from many cultures. God has given us living pictures to walk through in life. He meant for us to get along. One of the most insecure statements that I hear from people is "I do not have any friends." Another is "I don't need friends." Some even have the nerve to end the statement with "I have Jesus. That is all I need, really."

In the beginning, God created the earth. On the sixth day, He created man, and He saw that man needed a companion, so he created woman from man. Now, that is something. God almighty saw that we needed somebody other than ourselves on earth. When Jesus started His mission on earth, He chose twelve disciples to help Him accomplish the mission. He could have done it alone, but He chose others to help accomplish the task of pulling souls out of the fire. I am so glad that He loved them unconditionally, even those He knew would betray Him. Billions of people live on earth, and all, I believe, were made in God's image, breathing the breath of God.

Get to the root of your distrust and disbelief in people. People can and will hurt you; I am not saying you should keep all of them in your life, but you must learn to trust people. Some will hurt you intentionally, and some will hurt you unintentionally. If your practice is to cut off everybody who hurts your feelings or owes you money, you may end up very alone and bitter. It won't be as devastating as when you stop trusting God. Yet, it will affect your life and the lives of others who are a part of your life.

"I am the vine, ye are the branches: He that abideth in me, and I in him, the same bringeth forth much fruit: for without me ye can do nothing" (John 15:5). This scripture is saying that the branch is going to have a hard time bearing fruit without the vine. Jesus is the vine, and we are the branches. The world needs Jesus; your family needs you. Are you the vine in your family? Are family branches being impacted by you?

At my mother's funeral, I sat and looked at her. She looked so beautiful. I thought about how my dear friend Vi and I had gone shopping for a suit for Mom to wear; we had to shop laying the dresses or suits down because this outfit would be for a person lying down. I thought about how grateful to God I was when I realized that I had a beautiful suit in my closet that still had the tags on it. My mother loved that suit when she saw it in my store. Then I looked around at my sisters; each one of them has a beautiful feature taken from Mom. My youngest sister sang one of my mother's favorite songs; she stood so regally and sang with such dignity. Our mother was proud of her girls that day. Then, for a moment, I became angry, terribly irate.

Behind us sat some of my mom's immediate family, her brothers and their families and a few nieces and nephews. My brother's former wife even attended. I thought that was honorable of her. But I wanted to slap each one them, maybe even kick a few of them, because not one of them had visited her, and I found out that most didn't even know that she'd been sick and had been gone from her home for seven years. She loved her family—at least she sounded as though she did. They loved her. Yet no one was willing to bury whatever family issues had kept the family apart. I do know from hearing through the grapevine that someone owed somebody money and one of them took a piece of land from somebody—madness is what I heard most of my life. Therefore, the children of the major vines and roots could not connect, because you love your vine and you always, no matter what, want to keep the major vine happy. Consequently, you would rather leave the other branches alone.

I do not believe there is anyone on earth who knows that he or she has family and does not feel the family connection. I wondered what my mom's family was thinking when they watched her lying in that coffin. I wondered what they were thinking when they lowered her into the ground. So much time had been wasted, so many moments unspoken.

Fortunately we connected and often reach out to each other. For the older generation, it will probably never be a total connection, but I pray that the generation behind us will do better. How can we say that we love the Lord, trust Him, and appreciate how faithful He is and then hate, distrust, and put conditions on the very people He gave to us? He gave you your family, or He allowed you to have that family.

Stop the madness, people, and get it straight. We have wandered in the wilderness too long. It is not about you; it is about your generation, and it is about our universe. There are too many angry folks in this world, and it starts somewhere. I almost bet that it started with behaviors in the immediate families. Our families are losing faith in God and in each other.

On the left side of my brain, I began to think differently once we arrived at my house after my mother's funeral. I watched different people eating, laughing, and talking; we hugged each other, and we were very happy to be together. Her family was extremely appreciative that they were a part of this moment. My anger turned to joy. How happy I was to see my mom's family there for her and her children. It was too late for Mom, but it was a blessing for us.

Then again, blame flooded my soul. As we played a game of Taboo, I thought to myself, *Why did I not call them? Why did I choose not to include them in my mother's tragedy?* I had not reached out to them either. Do you see how the madness was beginning to start all over with me?

We have a choice to heal or to remain ill. It is an illness when we allow the twists and turns in life to stagnate our lives. Whatever they did, you repent and then forgive, and you keep life moving. If for some reason your heart is cold now, encourage those coming after you to connect to their family roots. Nothing can take the place of sisters or brothers. It feels great to be able to say "Uncle" and "Auntie," and it is a lot of fun to hang out with Cousin Joe. Houses, cars, land—stuff will never be able to replace people. Remember this—social media (it's wonderful) will never be able to replace the voice, touch, hug, or warmth of a human being. Family matters and everything that each family chooses to do affect the world. Whatever you go through, stop the madness. Just have faith!

Do you allow sin to enter your home? I would like to expound a little on this question because too often we do. Actually, we do not even see what we are doing as sinful. I am going to use my family as an example. For many years, traveling in the military, we had parties. In our minds, we felt like if no one was cursing, fighting, or sexing it up, all was good, not understanding that alcohol was being associated with fun; therefore, one of the main things that wipe out so many family members was being served to the people we loved. Alcohol can become as addictive as drugs. It was a generational curse on my family, and I did not even see it. That curse has been broken in the name of Jesus, and we won't have to deal with it in the generations to come.

Often as Christians, we say we cannot judge, because we all have sinned—you know what we say. Then we sit back and watch folks do all kinds of things, some in the name of Jesus. Stop the madness, and stop some of these horrible things from happening in your presence. We are seeking after Christ, spreading the gospel, and pulling folks out of the fire. Start with your family. Do whatever you do with kindness, but do not conform to things that you know to be ungodly. Begin attempting to transform the wickedness around you. We want to be in perfect peace, and we want our families to be in perfect peace. You will always influence someone else's life; it is never only about you. Trust in God, and just have faith!

There is a story about this in the Bible, found in the book of Genesis (by the way, did I tell you earlier how fascinating the book of Genesis is?). Jacob and Esau were brothers; their father's name was Isaac. Jacob seemed to be a mama's boy. He did not do too much hard work—at least this is how I interpreted it. Esau was a hunter and outdoorsman, always working, and Isaac loved his food. Esau was in line for his father's blessing. He came out of the field one day, tired and hungry, and sold his birthright to his brother Jacob for lentil stew. Isaac ended up giving Jacob his blessing before going on to glory. The food was a part of the story. Jacob and his mom had some tricks going on too. Read the story in Genesis 25:29–34 and Genesis 27:30–40. Esau was hot when he found out that his dad had given his birthright to his brother. I do not know why, because he had sold his birthright to his brother for stew.

Instant gratification is another thing that keeps families in a hot mess. We cause our own problems and then get mad at everybody in the family because he or she does not play into our dysfunctions. Esau would not have starved; he needed to wait an hour or two before eating. You will be all right without the new clothes, car, home, or trip to the islands. Debt destroys marriages, and instant gratification causes problems. Lifetime anger with family members separates families, and unbelief gives control to the devil. Stop the madness.

I need you to do something, because I am seeing too many strange things happening in our world. First, follow peace with all people and holiness (pursue consecration and holiness); then exercise foresight (looking diligently), and be on the watch too (look after one another). *Look after one another.* I cannot stress this one enough. Let others help you with your children; listen to what they say. Do not let the babies have everything and all things without teaching them some things about life.

Do not pursue instant gratification as Esau did; you will lose something. You can lose your mind. You never know how folks get what they get. Be thankful for what you have. Trust in God. He will always provide for you, providing that you are obedient to His word. You always have to have action in order to cause action. Resentment, bitterness, and hatred cause trouble and bitter torment, and the many become contaminated and corrupted by it. Do you want to be a part of contaminating folks around you? Shame on you if you answer, "Whatever," or "It is on them."

We really need to turn the flow of hatred around in this world; I believe it starts with the family and with the people we meet. Each person affects other people in one way or another. How are you affecting people, good or bad?

Have faith, and allow God to purge things out of you. Allow Him to prune you, and continue your walk with God. Look to God and bury the madness in your life. If you smell like a bed of roses already, help pull someone else out of his or her madness. If you feel like the person won't allow you to help, begin to pray for him or her daily with a sincere prayer from your heart. We all need rescuing at some point in our lives. We must stop turning our heads and joining in on those things we know will destroy our family, friends, coworkers, and ourselves.

I have been talking to a young man whom I love dearly, and I found out that at a very early age, he felt like no one loved him. He felt that he was in this world all alone. As close as I was to this person, I would not have ever guessed that he felt this way. He was family. He laughed, he played jokes, and he was always running around like a happy camper. Yet in the very early stages of his life, he was destining his life for chaos and destruction. God had other plans for this young man. He had gifted him with great looks, a beautiful voice, and gifted hands to build, cook, and just about anything he needed to do to make a very good living and to be able to help others. He allowed his mind to wander in a dark state. This led him to separate from his family and friends for many years. His life was in disarray. His mind was always in a state of confusion. It took him many years to see the light.

Let us start taking a closer look at our family members. Let us start listening to them—I mean *really listening* to them. We won't see all the signs, and we won't know all their sorrows or joys, but if we do not slow down with the busy moments in our lives, we are going to continue to lose our family and friends without having a clue of what happened.

I have a brother who, at the time of writing, I have not seen in years. I do not know if he is dead or alive. We were in contact for maybe a year several years ago, and then we lost contact. My husband and I tried contacting him many times. We could not contact him even when our mother died. What a misfortune, growing up with a blood relative and not even knowing if he is dead or alive in this world! Do you see why it is so important that we stop the madness and begin pulling our families into the light?

I know some of you have many friends and could not care less about family, but how can you be a true friend if you cannot love your own? They may have issued you some deep hurt, I know, but you had better try. Start with prayer, and if possible add fasting with your praying to help break the strongholds.

Fasting is interesting, and it is not something that I comprehended in my earlier life. If you see me, do not ask me why; I do not know. Still, I know prayer and fasting works. I do not advise you to fast without understanding the concept. So find yourself a good book to read on fasting. I suggest *Fasting* by Jentezen Franklin.[1] It is an easy read; it will take you one day to read with understanding. Once you understand the power of fasting and praying, do it for yourself and your family. Again, we must start breaking these strongholds off our lives and off our family's lives.

Unbelief and self-gratification will lead to behaviors that can lead to you missing eternal life, which is our utmost birthright and purpose. We see on a daily basis how bitterness, distrust, and anger destroy families and the things around us. These things not only destroy families; they are destroying our communities, cities, states, and country. We have madness in every form; we must begin to trust in God and just have faith that He is our shepherd and we shall not want!

Chapter 7

MINISTRY AND FAITH
(JUST HAVE FAITH)

Do you ever wonder what your purpose is on this earth? Were you called by God but you really do not feel like accepting the call? Do you spread the gospel? Do you believe Genesis 1? Do you believe that you are fit for the fight? Do you know that you are in the darkness and kind of like it? You hear the word *ministry* all the time. Have you asked yourself what it is? Do you spread the gospel? Do you believe that Jesus is returning? When you take your last breath, will you be ready to have a little talk with Jesus?

There are many meanings for the word *ministry*; for this book, I prefer to use the meaning documented in *Merriam-Webster's Collegiate Dictionary*:[1] "the office, duties, or functions of a minister; the body of ministers of religion; Clergy; a person or thing through which something is accomplished." However, many claim that ministry is an act of serving. This is the one meaning that I would like to sink into your mind. We are not serving enough in this world. I am not sure how we ended up so wrapped up in a pool of me, I, and I got mine, but we had better stop it!

I believe that we do a fantastic job giving money to specific causes, especially if it is convenient or worthy of the media. Do not take what I am saying the wrong way; do not dare stop giving. What I am saying is that we must begin to start serving with our time and our physical efforts. I believe the last time that I went out to serve food to the homeless and others it was a major event near my home. Although I give money faithfully, I am finding that I do not give my time as faithfully.

We were eating in one of the well-known establishments one afternoon, and I noticed a few elderly women sitting alone eating; now they may have been perfectly happy, but there was one whom my spirit was urging me to ask to sit with us. None of us had our food at the time. I did not act upon it, because it was so awkward. God's thoughts and actions are not like ours. This is what I seem to forget sometimes. It was not about me; it was about her. I thought about it the rest of that day, and it is obvious it still enters my mind. It would have been easy for me to pay for her meal, but it was so hard for me to ask her to fellowship with us. I do not have a problem with this type of scenario anymore, but that afternoon was a revelation for me.

Acts of kindness are a part of ministering to others; you do not have to be a minister to perform acts of kindness. Stop waiting for special events or disasters to happen before you give your time or before you are kind to others. There are people in every city who need your help. Sometimes that help is only a smile or a conversation.

We should be spreading the gospel, but we seem to be having a problem talking to each other. We are quick to speak when there is chaos among us, but a good clean conversation seems hard for people. We have gotten out of the habit of talking about things that are peaceful and righteous. How do we expect to spread the gospel and minister to God's children? Try getting your mind out of those reality shows and begin to check your reality. Is it good? Is it ministering to others? Let us start trusting in God's word! Have faith in Him. Every time we rely on ourselves, we fail someone.

"In the beginning God created the heaven and the earth" (Genesis

1:1). "And God saw every thing that he had made, and behold, it was very good. And the evening and the morning were the sixth day" (Genesis 1:31). Everything was very good—nature, men, women, birds, the ocean, and all the animals, *everything*. Guess whom God chose to take care of the earth. He chose human beings! In Genesis 1:28, it says, "God blessed the first man and woman and told them to be fruitful and multiply and fill the earth and subdue it, and have dominion over the fish of the sea and over the birds of the heavens and over every living thing that moves on the earth." Some may argue this issue; I won't argue with you. I believe that this is so, and I have faith in the Word of God.

You may be wondering what Genesis has to do with ministry and faith. Well, how can you spread the gospel or truly minister to others if you do not believe in the beginning? If you do not believe in the beginning, you are in denial about the rest of the Word. You know that you are in the darkness, but you have convinced yourself that it is all good because deep down inside you like what you are doing. One of my brothers told me, "Sis, I could hear the voice of God, but I wanted to do what I wanted. I thought that I was having fun." He spent one too many times in jail for this very reason. I never went to jail, but I spent one too many times in confusion and shamefulness for this very reason too.

Start committing to God's word, so that you can effectively minister to others; we need everyone to get onboard. It does not matter if you are a bishop, deacon, preacher, ordained elder, licensed minister, or evangelist. What matters is that you start helping others to come into the light. My brother has given me so much revelation on the importance of helping others with words and the Word and with giving your time.

These are some things that you can start doing to help minister to others. Call your family members, love and like unconditionally, seek out your neighbors, or go out with an evangelism team and support their efforts. Become more active in your church; join a church; help an organization that serve the homeless, the elderly, or children; volunteer at a hospital or school; be kinder to your family; be kinder to yourself; implement an act of kindness toward someone every day; and so on. Find something different to do at least once a year or once a month. Trust God in everything that you do. Just have faith!

"And Jesus said unto him, No man, having put his hand to the plough, and looking back, is fit for the kingdom of God" (Luke 9:62). Y'all start committing to the Word. "Study to shew thyself approved unto God, a workman that needeth not to be ashamed, rightly dividing the word of truth" (2 Timothy 2:15). Stop looking back. I know that it is easier to remain with those things that are familiar, but often the familiar is not where we should be. We must move forward, and we have to begin to study God's word. How else are we going to model God's ways and His character? People are watching you. People you do not even know are watching you. Oh my, another discovery! In some cases, you are indirectly ministering to folks, and you do not even know it.

What impact are you making on those people who watch you and listen to you from a distance? Get out of your hectic existence; you are making time for everything but the Word. You are probably saying, "I have too much to do. I have the kids. I have to cook. I have to get myself together. I am still out clubbing and drinking. I just do not have time." What if God decides that He does not have time for you? What if you are missing an assignment from God that will thrust you into another dominion, cancel all your debts, and cause your family members and future generations to become extra blessed and you miss it all because of your busy lifestyle and your disbelief?

I know someone reading this book is going to say, "I am busy, but I believe, really." I thought the same thing about myself until I really began to get into the Word of God. A shift begins to happen and continues the more you study, pray, and praise. I want you to experience that shift. It is wonderful, and it is peaceful. Stop here for a few minutes; ask God to increase your faith and to increase your wisdom in time management. Ask Him to take away your strongholds, so that you may get busy ministering to His people. Trust him, and just have faith!

Understand your calling. "And he gave some, apostles; and some, prophets; and some evangelists; and some, pastors and teachers; for the perfecting of the saints, for the work of the ministry, for the edifying of the body of Christ" (Ephesians 4:11–12). If you are called to one of these ministries, put on the overall armor of God, so that you can stand against the trickeries of the devil. You are going to need this in order to fight the good fight and minister. Read Ephesians 6:11 about putting on the armor of God.

A friend and I were talking one day, and she was telling me about a preacher who had made the comment that Christians are working too hard trying to look like the world. It was such a profound statement, and it got me to thinking. The world should be seeking after this little light of mine. Christians should be shining so brightly that others would want what we have.

We use more analogies over the pulpit and in our conversations. We have used R&B artists' lyrics, and we have even resorted to using gangster slang to help get our points across. We act as though God's words are not sufficient. I have even heard a few folks uttering out of their mouths that we are going to make Jesus famous. Are they kidding? Jesus was famous before we entered our mother's womb! We are having more dances and entertainment in the church, which is the place of worship rather than a nightclub. Folks, we have work to do! We must get back to the business of spreading the gospel. Trust God, and just have faith!

If you truly trust God and have faith in His Word, then know that all we have to do is water the seed and God will do the rest. We mean well, but in actuality, we are confusing folks. I attended a gospel concert last year; it vexed my soul. Tears were streaming out of my eyes. My friends were stunned too. I have not been interested in attending another since. The DJ would play club music one minute and then a gospel song the next. Folks were singing Al Green and Luther Vandross; then he would play a dance song, and folks would get up dancing. After they danced for a few minutes, he went back to the gospel. Throughout all that, they would say we need to learn how to have fun. People, we need to learn how to worship!

His grace is sufficient! During Paul's semiconfinement in Rome, he wrote to many groups and individuals. His letters consist of many of the final chapters of the New Testament. His epistles are full of spiritual advice from which many of the basic elements of Christian belief were drawn. Paul is an interesting character. He used to persecute Christians until he had an encounter with God. God can use anybody: drunks, drug users, procrastinators, thieves, liars, murderers, *anybody*. Allow Him to pull you into the light. Let your light shine. There is a holy thing inside of you.

Because of His unconditional love for us (even when we were dead in trespasses), He made us alive in Christ (by grace we have been saved). In addition, He raised us up together and made us sit together in the heavenly places in Christ Jesus, that in the ages to come He might show the exceeding riches of His grace (unmerited favor) in His kindness toward us in Christ Jesus (Ephesians 2:4–7 and Romans 3:21).

What does it mean to be seated together in the heavenly places in Christ Jesus? We are in a position of rest in Jesus's finished work. To be seated in Christ is to rest, to trust in Him. God wants us to receive everything our Savior has accomplished on our behalf. God wants us to take the position of relying on Jesus and stop relying on ourselves.

Some may ask, "Can I save myself?" The answer is no. Christians are saved by grace. The grace of God is the source of salvation; faith is the channel. God alone saves. Salvation never originates in the efforts of people; it always arises out of the loving-kindness of God. Take the time to read Ephesians 2:8–10. The love of God for His children was demonstrated through Jesus's work on the cross on our behalf. Rest in Jesus's finished work. His grace is sufficient. Accept Him, trust Him, and just have faith!

If you repent of your sin and then confess and trust Jesus Christ as your Lord and Savior, you will be saved from your sins! Read this, stop, and meditate on it. "For whoever calls on the name of the Lord shall be saved" (Romans 10:13). "If you confess with your mouth the Lord Jesus and believe in your heart that God has raised Him from the dead, you will be saved. For with the heart one believes unto righteousness, and with the mouth confession is made unto salvation" (Romans 10:9–10).

Not that many years ago—I believe my son was in college at the time—I was getting into my Word. I remember my son needing answers regarding being saved. I distinctly remember how I panicked. This was my son. No way did I want to lead him on the wrong track. I was already feeling like I had failed him along the way spiritually. I am a good mother, but as far as introducing my son to Jesus the way my mom introduced me, I do not believe that happened. Rather than panicking, all I had to tell him was to repent his sins and then confess and trust Jesus Christ as his Lord and Savior!

Do not make your Christian walk complicated. When you get into the Word, you will see that there are some basic things that you must do and all else will follow. I am not sure if this quick reference source is still available, but Dr. David Jeremiah compiled a quick reference guide called *Walking Down the Romans Road*.[2] It is a guide for sharing your faith. I found this guide after I had that brief conversation with my son; I would be ready to answer that question immediately from that point forward. I was ready to minister to those seeking to be saved.

As I am having this written conversation with you, I thought about the promise in the beginning to Israel (Deuteronomy 30:9–10). Moses tells the Israelites that: "God will make thee plenteous in every work of thine hand. In the fruit of thy body, and in the fruit of thy cattle, and in the fruit of thy land, for good, Then he will rejoice over thee for good, as he rejoiced over thy fathers." Fast-forward: "Now unto him that is able to do exceeding abundantly above all that we ask or think, according to the power that worketh in us. Unto him be glory in the church by Christ Jesus through-out all ages, world without end. Amen" (Ephesians 3:20–21).

We are the heirs to these promises. Do you have faith in His word? We were not there. We either believe His word or not. "God is not a man that he should lie; neither the son of man that he should repent: hath he said, and shall he not do it? Or hath he spoken, and shall he not make it good?" (Numbers 23:19). Just have faith!

There are a few insights given by Moses in Deuteronomy 30:10, regarding what the people of Israel should continue to do. "If thou shalt hearken [listen, give an ear to], the voice of the LORD thy God, to keep his commandments and his statutes which are written in this book of the law, and if thou turn unto the LORD thy God with all thine heart, and with all thy soul."

"So then faith cometh by hearing, and hearing by the word of God" (Romans 10:17). Have we stopped listening to God? Are we turning to Him with all our hearts and souls? Are we still trusting Him and having faith in His word and His promises? Jesus got the job done for us. Why do we continue to act as though He did not take it all to the cross?

> Surely he hath borne our griefs, and carried our sorrows; yet we did esteem him stricken, smitten of God, and afflicted. But he was wounded for our transgressions [wrongdoings, misbehaviors, offenses, misdemeanors, disobediences]; he was bruised for our iniquities [immorality, crimes, sin, wickedness, and problems]: the chastisement [discipline, reprimand, rebuke, correction] of our peace was upon him; and with his stripes, we are healed. (Isaiah 53:4–5)

> The LORD shall open unto thee his good treasure, the heaven to give the rain unto thy land in his season, and to bless all the work of thine hand, and thou shalt lend unto many nations, and thou shalt not borrow. And the LORD shall make thee the head, and not the tail; and thou shalt be above only, and thou shalt not be beneath; if that thou hearken unto the commandments of the LORD thy God, which I command thee this day, to observe and to do them: (YHVH). Does he promise and not fulfill? (Deuteronomy 28:12–13)

Do you have faith that you are an inheritor to this promise? I always hear folks saying, "I am the head and not the tail; I am the lender and not the borrower." Do you really believe what you say? I am ministering to you; we must get this down in our soul. We are overspending and overanalyzing, and we are losing hope in what was already done for us at the cross. Trust in the Lord, and just have faith!

Take the time to read Habakkuk (it is only three chapters long). It describes the state that some of us are in today. The book of Habakkuk is a conversation between the prophet and God. Habakkuk was appealing to God to end injustice on earth. I believe this book alone will minister to your spirit. Two questions concerned Habakkuk. One was why God allowed wicked people to prosper without being punished (the leaders of Judah oppressed the poor).

According to the Word, God answered: the Chaldeans (Babylonians) would come to punish Judah. This answer Habakkuk was not expecting. He then asked why a just God would use a country even more sinful to punish his people. God answered that the Babylonians would also be punished once they had accomplished His purpose. Habakkuk trusted God's ways!

Do we trust God's ways when we see all the mess going on in our world today? Like Judah, if they do not conform to God's will, they can only expect punishment and destruction as a nation. When we cannot see healing or feel healing, we should trust God. Even though we see destruction in America and other countries, we shall continue to rejoice in the Lord, continue to share God's word with others, and just have faith!

If we do not conform to God's will, we can only expect chaos in our lives and in our hearts. In addition, if our nation continues to conform to the world and continues our wicked ways, America should anticipate punishment and destruction. We continue to experience diseases, acts like 9/11, and an increase in the lack of respect for authority and no respect for ourselves in some instances. Ask God to speak to our hearts, and listen to what He has to say. Stop leaving ministry up to our leaders, and begin helping them to help others. First, get yourself together. God trusts you to get it together and help Him on earth as in Heaven. Do not wait until you become perfect; it probably won't happen immediately. Ask God to speak to your heart and to your spirit, trust Him, and just have faith.

I am requesting another call to action. Start trusting and believing in God. Have faith in what He places in your heart, soul, and spirit. He does not love me any more than He loves you. He does not love your bishop or pastor any more than He loves the homeless person living under the bridge. He wants us to love. How else can we effectively minister to each other and to other lost souls? It is time for us to get ourselves together and begin to help each other one by one, day by day! Please stop conforming to those things that you know are not right and start transforming into righteousness. Start studying His Word; the Word was inspired by God (2 Timothy 3:16). I am sure that we have questions just like Habakkuk. We also get angry when we see senseless crimes being committed. We need to believe and trust in God, no matter what we see and hear. We do not have to use Satan's tactics to draw God's children; water the seed with love and God's Word, and God will do the rest. Just have faith.

The last illustration in this book is probably one of the most profound pictures of all the illustrations throughout the book. I say this because the Word says, "So then faith cometh by hearing, and hearing by the word of God" (Romans 10:17). Then 2 Timothy 3:16 says, "All scripture is given by inspiration of God, and is profitable for doctrine, for reproof, for correction, or instruction in righteousness." Knowing that the Word was/is inspired by God and it is a manual for the way we should live, quicken your spirit to hear the Word, read the Word, and keep it written. You cannot effectively minister to others if you do not know or have an understanding of the Word of God. Trust in the Lord. Believe and receive His Word. Just have faith.

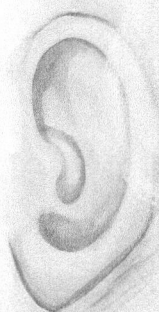

Conclusion

What should you do when you cannot see what you hope for? The answer to this question is that you must continue to have faith in God. Each chapter in this book consists of a journey that has increased my spiritual growth in wisdom, knowledge, stature, and favor with God and with man.

Study the Word of God, so when you encounter trials and obstacles in your life, you will have a solid foundation to stand on (even when you waver). In addition, you will have a body of armor to destroy the enemy. Learn from your experiences; even though you want to move on from your past, do not let your experiences become faded memories. Your past will help you mature.

Each chapter in my life, including those chapters that I did not share, helped me to begin a spiritual journey seeking after the kingdom of God and His righteousness. Peace comes with seeking after God's character.

The Word is living and so powerful. Use the Word to help guide your life and to help you minister to God's children in earth. Share the Word with your family and friends and with strangers. You won't always have the answers, and life is not always going to be fair. To be honest, some twists and turns that life deals will not make sense at all. Still, through it all, trust in God. Trust His Word, and just have faith.

Scripture References

From the Old Testament

Genesis 1:1
In the beginning God created the heaven and the earth.

Genesis 1:3
And God said, Let there be light: and there was light.

Genesis 1:28
And God blessed them, and God said unto them, Be fruitful, and multiply, and replenish the earth, and subdue it: and have dominion over the fish of the sea, and over the fowl of the air, and over every living thing that moveth upon the earth.

Genesis 1:31
And God saw every thing that he had made, and, behold, it was very good. And the evening and the morning were the sixth day.

Genesis 19:28
And he looked toward Sodom and Gomorrah, and toward all the land of the plain, and beheld, and, lo, the smoke of the country went up as the smoke of a furnace.

Genesis 21:2

For Sarah conceived, and bare Abraham a son in his old age, at the set
    time of which God had spoken to him.

Genesis 22:2–19

And he said, Take now thy son, thine only son Isaac, whom thou lovest,
    and get thee into the land of Moriah; and offer him there for a burnt
    offering upon one of the mountains which I will tell thee of.

And Abraham rose up early in the morning, and saddled his ass, and
    took two of his young men with him, and Isaac his son, and clave the
    wood for the burnt offering, and rose up, and went unto the place of
    which God had told him.

Then on the third day Abraham lifted up his eyes, and saw the place
    afar off.

And Abraham said unto his young men, Abide ye here with the ass; and
    I and the lad will go yonder and worship, and come again to you.

And Abraham took the wood of the burnt offering, and laid it upon Isaac
    his son; and he took the fire in his hand, and a knife; and they went
    both of them together.

And Isaac spake unto Abraham his father, and said, My father: and he
    said, Here am I, my son. And he said, Behold the fire and the wood:
    but where is the lamb for a burnt offering?

And Abraham said, My son, God will provide himself a lamb for a burnt
    offering: so they went both of them together.

And they came to the place which God had told him of; and Abraham
    built an altar there, and laid the wood in order, and bound Isaac his
    son, and laid him on the altar upon the wood.

And Abraham stretched forth his hand, and took the knife to slay his son.

And the angel of the Lord called unto him out of heaven, and said,
    Abraham, Abraham: and he said, Here am I.

And he said, Lay not thine hand upon the lad, neither do thou any thing
    unto him: for now I know that thou fearest God, seeing thou hast
    not withheld thy son, thine only son from me.

And Abraham lifted up his eyes, and looked, and behold behind him a
ram caught in a thicket by his horns: and Abraham went and took the
ram, and offered him up for a burnt offering in the stead of his son.

And Abraham called the name of that place Jehovah-jireh: as it is said to
this day, In the mount of the LORD it shall be seen.

And the angel of the LORD called unto Abraham out of heaven the second
time,

And said, By myself have I sworn, saith the LORD, for because thou hast
done this thing, and

That in blessing I will bless thee, and in multiplying I will multiply thy
seed as the stars of the heaven, and as the sand which is upon the sea
shore; and thy seed shall possess the gate of his enemies;

And in thy seed shall all the nations of the earth be blessed; because thou
hast obeyed my voice.

So Abraham returned unto his young men, and they rose up and went
together to Beer-sheba; and Abraham dwelt at Beer-sheba.

Genesis 25:29–34

And Jacob sod pottage: and Esau came from the field, and he was faint:

And Esau said to Jacob, Feed me, I pray thee, with that same red pottage;
for I am faint: therefore was his name called Edom.

And Jacob said, Sell me this day thy birthright.

And Esau said, Behold, I am at the point to die: and what profit shall this
birthright do to me?

And Jacob said, Swear to me this day; and he sware unto him: and he
sold his birthright unto Jacob.

Then Jacob gave Esau bread and pottage of lentiles; and he did eat
and drink, and rose up, and went his way: thus Esau despised his
birthright.

Genesis 27:30–40

And it came to pass, as soon as Isaac had made an end of blessing Jacob, and Jacob was yet scarce gone out from the presence of Isaac his father, that Esau his brother came in from his hunting.

And he also had made savoury meat, and brought it unto his father, and said unto his father, Let my father arise, and eat of his son's venison, that thy soul may bless me.

And Isaac his father said unto him, Who art thou? And he said, I am thy son, thy firstborn Esau.

And Isaac trembled very exceedingly, and said, Who? where is he that hath taken venison, and brought it me, and I have eaten of all before thou camest, and have blessed him? yea, and he shall be blessed.

And when Esau heard the words of his father, he cried with a great and exceeding bitter cry, and said unto his father, Bless me, even me also, O my father.

And he said, Thy brother came with subtilty, and hath taken away thy blessing.

And he said, Is not he rightly named Jacob? for he hath supplanted me these two times: he took away my birthright; and, behold, now he hath taken away my blessing. And he said, Hast thou not reserved a blessing for me?

And Isaac answered and said unto Esau, Behold, I have made him thy lord, and all his brethren have I given to him for servants; and with corn and wine have I sustained him: and what shall I do now unto thee, my son?

And Esau said unto his father, Hast thou but one blessing, my father? bless me, even me also, O my father. And Esau lifted up his voice, and wept.

And Isaac his father answered and said unto him, Behold, thy dwelling shall be the fatness of the earth, and of the dew of heaven from above;

And by thy sword shalt thou live, and shalt serve thy brother; and it shall come to pass when thou shalt have the dominion, that thou shalt break his yoke from off thy neck.

Genesis 37:24

And they took him, and cast him into a pit: and the pit was empty, there was no water in it.

Genesis 49:11

Binding his foal unto the vine, and his ass's colt unto the choice vine; he washed his garments in wine, and his clothes in the blood of grapes:

Exodus 10:1–15

And the Lord said unto Moses, Go in unto Pharaoh: for I have hardened his heart, and the heart of his servants, that I might shew these my signs before him:

And that thou mayest tell in the ears of thy son, and of thy son's son, what things I have wrought in Egypt, and my signs which I have done among them; that ye may know how that I am the Lord.

And Moses and Aaron came in unto Pharaoh, and said unto him, Thus saith the Lord God of the Hebrews, How long wilt thou refuse to humble thyself before me? let my people go, that they may serve me.

Else, if thou refuse to let my people go, behold, to morrow will I bring the locusts into thy coast:

And they shall cover the face of the earth, that one cannot be able to see the earth: and they shall eat the residue of that which is escaped, which remaineth unto you from the hail, and shall eat every tree which groweth for you out of the field:

And they shall fill thy houses, and the houses of all thy servants, and the houses of all the Egyptians; which neither thy fathers, nor thy fathers' fathers have seen, since the day that they were upon the earth unto this day. And he turned himself, and went out from Pharaoh.

And Pharaoh's servants said unto him, How long shall this man be a snare unto us? let the men go, that they may serve the Lord their God: knowest thou not yet that Egypt is destroyed?

And Moses and Aaron were brought again unto Pharaoh: and he said unto them, Go, serve the Lord your God: but who are they that shall go?

And Moses said, We will go with our young and with our old, with our sons and with our daughters, with our flocks and with our herds will we go; for we must hold a feast unto the Lord.

And he said unto them, Let the Lord be so with you, as I will let you go, and your little ones: look to it; for evil is before you.

Not so: go now ye that are men, and serve the Lord; for that ye did desire. And they were driven out from Pharaoh's presence.

And the Lord said unto Moses, Stretch out thine hand over the land of Egypt for the locusts, that they may come up upon the land of Egypt, and eat every herb of the land, even all that the hail hath left.

And Moses stretched forth his rod over the land of Egypt, and the Lord brought an east wind upon the land all that day, and all that night; and when it was morning, the east wind brought the locusts.

And the locust went up over all the land of Egypt, and rested in all the coasts of Egypt: very grievous were they; before them there were no such locusts as they, neither after them shall be such.

For they covered the face of the whole earth, so that the land was darkened; and they did eat every herb of the land, and all the fruit of the trees which the hail had left: and there remained not any green thing in the trees, or in the herbs of the field, through all the land of Egypt.

Exodus 19:18

And mount Sinai was altogether on a smoke, because the Lord descended upon it in fire: and the smoke thereof ascended as the smoke of a furnace, and the whole mount quaked greatly.

Exodus 24:4–8

And Moses wrote all the words of the Lord, and rose up early in the morning, and builded an altar under the hill, and twelve pillars, according to the twelve tribes of Israel.

And he sent young men of the children of Israel, which offered burnt offerings, and sacrificed peace offerings of oxen unto the LORD.

And Moses took half of the blood, and put it in basons; and half of the blood he sprinkled on the altar.

And he took the book of the covenant, and read in the audience of the people: and they said, All that the LORD hath said will we do, and be obedient.

And Moses took the blood, and sprinkled it on the people, and said, Behold the blood of the covenant, which the LORD hath made with you concerning all these words.

Numbers 23:19

God is not a man, that he should lie; neither the son of man, that he should repent: hath he said, and shall he not do it? or hath he spoken, and shall he not make it good?

Deuteronomy 17:2–6

If there be found among you, within any of thy gates which the LORD thy God giveth thee, man or woman, that hath wrought wickedness in the sight of the LORD thy God, in transgressing his covenant,

And hath gone and served other gods, and worshipped them, either the sun, or moon, or any of the host of heaven, which I have not commanded;

And it be told thee, and thou hast heard of it, and enquired diligently, and, behold, it be true, and the thing certain, that such abomination is wrought in Israel:

Then shalt thou bring forth that man or that woman, which have committed that wicked thing, unto thy gates, even that man or that woman, and shalt stone them with stones, till they die.

At the mouth of two witnesses, or three witnesses, shall he that is worthy of death be put to death; but at the mouth of one witness he shall not be put to death.

Deuteronomy 28:12–13

The LORD shall open unto thee his good treasure, the heaven to give the
   rain unto thy land in his season, and to bless all the work of thine
   hand: and thou shalt lend unto many nations, and thou shalt not
   borrow.

And the LORD shall make thee the head, and not the tail; and thou shalt
   be above only, and thou shalt not be beneath; if that thou hearken
   unto the commandments of the LORD thy God, which I command
   thee this day, to observe and to do them:

Deuteronomy 30:9–10

And the LORD thy God will make thee plenteous in every work of thine
   hand, in the fruit of thy body, and in the fruit of thy cattle, and in the
   fruit of thy land, for good: for the LORD will again rejoice over thee
   for good, as he rejoiced over thy fathers:

If thou shalt hearken unto the voice of the LORD thy God, to keep his
   commandments and his statutes which are written in this book of
   the law, and if thou turn unto the LORD thy God with all thine heart,
   and with all thy soul.

Job 3:21

Which long for death, but it cometh not; and dig for it more than for
   hid treasures;

Psalm 34:4

I sought the LORD, and he heard me, and delivered me from all my fears.

Psalm 40:2

He brought me up also out of an horrible pit, out of the miry clay, and set
   my feet upon a rock, and established my goings.

Psalm 73:25

Whom have I in heaven but thee? and there is none upon earth that I desire beside thee.

Psalm 89:27

Also I will make him my firstborn, higher than the kings of the earth.

Psalm 110:1

The LORD said unto my Lord, Sit thou at my right hand, until I make thine enemies thy footstool.

Psalm 116:10

I believed, therefore have I spoken: I was greatly afflicted:

Proverbs 13:12

Hope deferred maketh the heart sick: but when the desire cometh, it is a tree of life.

Isaiah 2:10–22

Enter into the rock, and hide thee in the dust, for fear of the LORD, and for the glory of his majesty.

The lofty looks of man shall be humbled, and the haughtiness of men shall be bowed down, and the LORD alone shall be exalted in that day.

For the day of the LORD of hosts shall be upon every one that is proud and lofty, and upon every one that is lifted up; and he shall be brought low:

And upon all the cedars of Lebanon, that are high and lifted up, and upon all the oaks of Bashan,

And upon all the high mountains, and upon all the hills that are lifted up,

And upon every high tower, and upon every fenced wall,

And upon all the ships of Tarshish, and upon all pleasant pictures.

And the loftiness of man shall be bowed down, and the haughtiness of men shall be made low: and the LORD alone shall be exalted in that day.

And the idols he shall utterly abolish.

And they shall go into the holes of the rocks, and into the caves of the
earth, for fear of the Lord, and for the glory of his majesty, when he
ariseth to shake terribly the earth.

In that day a man shall cast his idols of silver, and his idols of gold, which
they made each one for himself to worship, to the moles and to the
bats;

To go into the clefts of the rocks, and into the tops of the ragged rocks,
for fear of the Lord, and for the glory of his majesty, when he ariseth
to shake terribly the earth.

Cease ye from man, whose breath is in his nostrils: for wherein is he to
be accounted of?

Isaiah 5:21–25

Woe unto them that are wise in their own eyes, and prudent in their
own sight!

Woe unto them that are mighty to drink wine, and men of strength to
mingle strong drink:

Which justify the wicked for reward, and take away the righteousness of
the righteous from him!

Therefore as the fire devoureth the stubble, and the flame consumeth the
chaff, so their root shall be as rottenness, and their blossom shall go
up as dust: because they have cast away the law of the Lord of hosts,
and despised the word of the Holy One of Israel.

Therefore is the anger of the Lord kindled against his people, and he
hath stretched forth his hand against them, and hath smitten them:
and the hills did tremble, and their carcases were torn in the midst
of the streets. For all this his anger is not turned away, but his hand
is stretched out still.

Isaiah 13:6

Howl ye; for the day of the Lord is at hand; it shall come as a destruction
from the Almighty.

Isaiah 13:9–11

Behold, the day of the LORD cometh, cruel both with wrath and fierce anger, to lay the land desolate: and he shall destroy the sinners thereof out of it.

For the stars of heaven and the constellations thereof shall not give their light: the sun shall be darkened in his going forth, and the moon shall not cause her light to shine.

And I will punish the world for their evil, and the wicked for their iniquity; and I will cause the arrogancy of the proud to cease, and will lay low the haughtiness of the terrible.

Isaiah 24:21–23

And it shall come to pass in that day, that the LORD shall punish the host of the high ones that are on high, and the kings of the earth upon the earth.

And they shall be gathered together, as prisoners are gathered in the pit, and shall be shut up in the prison, and after many days shall they be visited.

Then the moon shall be confounded, and the sun ashamed, when the LORD of hosts shall reign in mount Zion, and in Jerusalem, and before his ancients gloriously.

Isaiah 26:20–21

Come, my people, enter thou into thy chambers, and shut thy doors about thee: hide thyself as it were for a little moment, until the indignation be overpast.

For, behold, the LORD cometh out of his place to punish the inhabitants of the earth for their iniquity: the earth also shall disclose her blood, and shall no more cover her slain.

Isaiah 34:1–4

Come near, ye nations, to hear; and hearken, ye people: let the earth hear, and all that is therein; the world, and all things that come forth of it.

For the indignation of the LORD is upon all nations, and his fury upon
all their armies: he hath utterly destroyed them, he hath delivered
them to the slaughter.

Their slain also shall be cast out, and their stink shall come up out of
their carcases, and the mountains shall be melted with their blood.

And all the host of heaven shall be dissolved, and the heavens shall be
rolled together as a scroll: and all their host shall fall down, as the
leaf falleth off from the vine, and as a falling fig from the fig tree.

Isaiah 34:8

For it is the day of the LORD's vengeance, and the year of recompences
for the controversy of Zion.

Isaiah 53:4–5

Surely he hath borne our griefs, and carried our sorrows: yet we did
esteem him stricken, smitten of God, and afflicted.

But he was wounded for our transgressions, he was bruised for our
iniquities: the chastisement of our peace was upon him; and with his
stripes we are healed.

Isaiah 63:1–3

Who is this that cometh from Edom, with dyed garments from Bozrah?
this that is glorious in his apparel, travelling in the greatness of his
strength? I that speak in righteousness, mighty to save.

Wherefore art thou red in thine apparel, and thy garments like him that
treadeth in the winefat?

I have trodden the winepress alone; and of the people there was none
with me: for I will tread them in mine anger, and trample them in
my fury; and their blood shall be sprinkled upon my garments, and
I will stain all my raiment.

Jeremiah 30:7

Alas! for that day is great, so that none is like it: it is even the time of Jacob's trouble; but he shall be saved out of it.

Jeremiah 33:3

Call unto me, and I will answer thee, and shew thee great and mighty things, which thou knowest not.

Ezekiel 1:1

Now it came to pass in the thirtieth year, in the fourth month, in the fifth day of the month, as I was among the captives by the river of Chebar, that the heavens were opened, and I saw visions of God.

Ezekiel 9:4

And the Lord said unto him, Go through the midst of the city, through the midst of Jerusalem, and set a mark upon the foreheads of the men that sigh and that cry for all the abominations that be done in the midst thereof.

Ezekiel 32:7–10

And when I shall put thee out, I will cover the heaven, and make the stars thereof dark; I will cover the sun with a cloud, and the moon shall not give her light.

All the bright lights of heaven will I make dark over thee, and set darkness upon thy land, saith the Lord God.

I will also vex the hearts of many people, when I shall bring thy destruction among the nations, into the countries which thou hast not known.

Yea, I will make many people amazed at thee, and their kings shall be horribly afraid for thee, when I shall brandish my sword before them; and they shall tremble at every moment, every man for his own life, in the day of thy fall.

Daniel 7:13

I saw in the night visions, and, behold, one like the Son of man came with the clouds of heaven, and came to the Ancient of days, and they brought him near before him.

Daniel 12:1

And at that time shall Michael stand up, the great prince which standeth for the children of thy people: and there shall be a time of trouble, such as never was since there was a nation even to that same time: and at that time thy people shall be delivered, every one that shall be found written in the book.

Hosea 10:8

The high places also of Aven, the sin of Israel, shall be destroyed: the thorn and the thistle shall come up on their altars; and they shall say to the mountains, Cover us; and to the hills, Fall on us.

Joel 2:10–11

The earth shall quake before them; the heavens shall tremble: the sun and the moon shall be dark, and the stars shall withdraw their shining:

And the Lord shall utter his voice before his army: for his camp is very great: for he is strong that executeth his word: for the day of the Lord is great and very terrible; and who can abide it?

Joel 2:28–32

And it shall come to pass afterward, that I will pour out my spirit upon all flesh; and your sons and your daughters shall prophesy, your old men shall dream dreams, your young men shall see visions:

And also upon the servants and upon the handmaids in those days will I pour out my spirit.

And I will shew wonders in the heavens and in the earth, blood, and fire, and pillars of smoke.

The sun shall be turned into darkness, and the moon into blood, before the great and terrible day of the Lord come.

And it shall come to pass, that whosoever shall call on the name of the Lord shall be delivered: for in mount Zion and in Jerusalem shall be deliverance, as the Lord hath said, and in the remnant whom the Lord shall call.

Amos 5:18

Woe unto you that desire the day of the Lord! to what end is it for you? the day of the Lord is darkness, and not light.

Habakkuk 1:1–17

The burden which Habakkuk the prophet did see.

O Lord, how long shall I cry, and thou wilt not hear! even cry out unto thee of violence, and thou wilt not save!

Why dost thou shew me iniquity, and cause me to behold grievance? for spoiling and violence are before me: and there are that raise up strife and contention.

Therefore the law is slacked, and judgment doth never go forth: for the wicked doth compass about the righteous; therefore wrong judgment proceedeth.

Behold ye among the heathen, and regard, and wonder marvelously: for I will work a work in your days, which ye will not believe, though it be told you.

For, lo, I raise up the Chaldeans, that bitter and hasty nation, which shall march through the breadth of the land, to possess the dwellingplaces that are not theirs.

They are terrible and dreadful: their judgment and their dignity shall proceed of themselves.

Their horses also are swifter than the leopards, and are more fierce than the evening wolves: and their horsemen shall spread themselves, and their horsemen shall come from far; they shall fly as the eagle that hasteth to eat.

They shall come all for violence: their faces shall sup up as the east wind, and they shall gather the captivity as the sand.

And they shall scoff at the kings, and the princes shall be a scorn unto them: they shall deride every strong hold; for they shall heap dust, and take it.

Then shall his mind change, and he shall pass over, and offend, imputing this his power unto his god.

Art thou not from everlasting, O Lord my God, mine Holy One? we shall not die. O Lord, thou hast ordained them for judgment; and, O mighty God, thou hast established them for correction.

Thou art of purer eyes than to behold evil, and canst not look on iniquity: wherefore lookest thou upon them that deal treacherously, and holdest thy tongue when the wicked devoureth the man that is more righteous than he?

And makest men as the fishes of the sea, as the creeping things, that have no ruler over them?

They take up all of them with the angle, they catch them in their net, and gather them in their drag: therefore they rejoice and are glad.

Therefore they sacrifice unto their net, and burn incense unto their drag; because by them their portion is fat, and their meat plenteous.

Shall they therefore empty their net, and not spare continually to slay the nations?

Zephaniah 1:15

That day is a day of wrath, a day of trouble and distress, a day of wasteness and desolation, a day of darkness and gloominess, a day of clouds and thick darkness …

Zephaniah 2:3

Seek ye the Lord, all ye meek of the earth, which have wrought his judgment; seek righteousness, seek meekness: it may be ye shall be hid in the day of the Lord's anger.

Zechariah 9:9

Rejoice greatly, O daughter of Zion; shout, O daughter of Jerusalem: behold, thy King cometh unto thee: he is just, and having salvation; lowly, and riding upon an ass, and upon a colt the foal of an ass.

Zechariah 9:11

As for thee also, by the blood of thy covenant I have sent forth thy prisoners out of the pit wherein is no water.

Zechariah 9:12–13

Turn you to the strong hold, ye prisoners of hope: even to day do I declare that I will render double unto thee;

When I have bent Judah for me, filled the bow with Ephraim, and raised up thy sons, O Zion, against thy sons, O Greece, and made thee as the sword of a mighty man.

Zechariah 12:10

And I will pour upon the house of David, and upon the inhabitants of Jerusalem, the spirit of grace and of supplications: and they shall look upon me whom they have pierced, and they shall mourn for him, as one mourneth for his only son, and shall be in bitterness for him, as one that is in bitterness for his firstborn.

Malachi 4:1

For, behold, the day cometh, that shall burn as an oven; and all the proud, yea, and all that do wickedly, shall be stubble: and the day that cometh shall burn them up, saith the Lord of hosts, that it shall leave them neither root nor branch.

From the New Testament

Matthew 3:12

Whose fan is in his hand, and he will throughly purge his floor, and gather his wheat into the garner; but he will burn up the chaff with unquenchable fire.

Matthew 7:7

Ask, and it shall be given you; seek, and ye shall find; knock, and it shall be opened unto you …

Matthew 7:8

For every one that asketh receiveth; and he that seeketh findeth; and to him that knocketh it shall be opened.

Matthew 17:20

And Jesus said unto them, Because of your unbelief: for verily I say unto you, If ye have faith as a grain of mustard seed, ye shall say unto this mountain, Remove hence to yonder place; and it shall remove; and nothing shall be impossible unto you.

Matthew 21:5

Tell ye the daughter of Sion, Behold, thy King cometh unto thee, meek, and sitting upon an ass, and a colt the foal of an ass.

Matthew 24:29

Immediately after the tribulation of those days shall the sun be darkened, and the moon shall not give her light, and the stars shall fall from heaven, and the powers of the heavens shall be shaken …

Matthew 26:64

Jesus saith unto him, Thou hast said: nevertheless I say unto you, Hereafter shall ye see the Son of man sitting on the right hand of power, and coming in the clouds of heaven.

Mark 11:22–24

And Jesus answering saith unto them, Have faith in God.

For verily I say unto you, That whosoever shall say unto this mountain, Be thou removed, and be thou cast into the sea; and shall not doubt in his heart, but shall believe that those things which he saith shall come to pass; he shall have whatsoever he saith.

Therefore I say unto you, What things soever ye desire, when ye pray, believe that ye receive them, and ye shall have them.

Luke 9:62

And Jesus said unto him, No man, having put his hand to the plough, and looking back, is fit for the kingdom of God.

Luke 17:6

And the Lord said, If ye had faith as a grain of mustard seed, ye might say unto this sycamine tree, Be thou plucked up by the root, and be thou planted in the sea; and it should obey you.

Luke 23:30

Then shall they begin to say to the mountains, Fall on us; and to the hills, Cover us.

John 12:14–15

And Jesus, when he had found a young ass, sat thereon; as it is written, Fear not, daughter of Sion: behold, thy King cometh, sitting on an ass's colt.

John 19:37

And again another scripture saith, They shall look on him whom they
  pierced.

Acts 2:17–21

And it shall come to pass in the last days, saith God, I will pour out of
  my Spirit upon all flesh: and your sons and your daughters shall
  prophesy, and your young men shall see visions, and your old men
  shall dream dreams:
And on my servants and on my handmaidens I will pour out in those
  days of my Spirit; and they shall prophesy:
And I will shew wonders in heaven above, and signs in the earth beneath;
  blood, and fire, and vapour of smoke:
The sun shall be turned into darkness, and the moon into blood, before
  the great and notable day of the Lord come:
And it shall come to pass, that whosoever shall call on the name of the
  Lord shall be saved.

Acts 2:34–35

For David is not ascended into the heavens: but he saith himself, The
  Lord said unto my Lord, Sit thou on my right hand,
Until I make thy foes thy footstool.

Romans 3:21

But now the righteousness of God without the law is manifested, being
  witnessed by the law and the prophets ...

Romans 3:24–25

Being justified freely by his grace through the redemption that is in
  Christ Jesus:
Whom God hath set forth to be a propitiation through faith in his blood,
  to declare his righteousness for the remission of sins that are past,
  through the forbearance of God ...

Romans 4:21

And being fully persuaded that, what he had promised, he was able also to perform.

Romans 8:28

And we know that all things work together for good to them that love God, to them who are the called according to his purpose.

Romans 8:37

Nay, in all these things we are more than conquerors through him that loved us.

Romans 10:9–10

That if thou shalt confess with thy mouth the Lord Jesus, and shalt believe in thine heart that God hath raised him from the dead, thou shalt be saved.
For with the heart man believeth unto righteousness; and with the mouth confession is made unto salvation.

Romans 10:13

For whosoever shall call upon the name of the Lord shall be saved.

Romans 10:17

So then faith cometh by hearing, and hearing by the word of God.

Romans 13:7–8

Render therefore to all their dues: tribute to whom tribute is due; custom to whom custom; fear to whom fear; honour to whom honour.
Owe no man any thing, but to love one another: for he that loveth another hath fulfilled the law.

1 Corinthians 11:25

After the same manner also he took the cup, when he had supped, saying, this cup is the new testament in my blood: this do ye, as oft as ye drink it, in remembrance of me.

1 Corinthians 15:25

For he must reign, till he hath put all enemies under his feet.

2 Corinthians 4:13–14

We having the same spirit of faith, according as it is written, I believed, and therefore have I spoken; we also believe, and therefore speak;

Knowing that he which raised up the Lord Jesus shall raise up us also by Jesus, and shall present us with you.

Galatians 3:22

But the scripture hath concluded all under sin, that the promise by faith of Jesus Christ might be given to them that believe.

Galatians 5:22–23

But the fruit of the Spirit is love, joy, peace, longsuffering, gentleness, goodness, faith,

Meekness, temperance: against such there is no law.

Ephesians 2:4–7

But God, who is rich in mercy, for his great love wherewith he loved us,

Even when we were dead in sins, hath quickened us together with Christ, (by grace ye are saved;)

And hath raised us up together, and made us sit together in heavenly places in Christ Jesus:

That in the ages to come he might shew the exceeding riches of his grace in his kindness toward us through Christ Jesus.

Ephesians 2:8–10

For by grace are ye saved through faith; and that not of yourselves: it is
the gift of God:

Not of works, lest any man should boast.

For we are his workmanship, created in Christ Jesus unto good works,
which God hath before ordained that we should walk in them.

Ephesians 3:10

To the intent that now unto the principalities and powers in heavenly
places might be known by the church the manifold wisdom of God ...

Ephesians 3:20–21

Now unto him that is able to do exceeding abundantly above all that we
ask or think, according to the power that worketh in us,

Unto him be glory in the church by Christ Jesus throughout all ages,
world without end. Amen.

Ephesians 4:11–12

And he gave some, apostles; and some, prophets; and some, evangelists;
and some, pastors and teachers; For the perfecting of the saints, for
the work of the ministry, for the edifying of the body of Christ ...

Ephesians 6:11

Put on the whole armour of God, that ye may be able to stand against
the wiles of the devil.

Ephesians 6:12

For we wrestle not against flesh and blood, but against principalities,
against powers, against the rulers of the darkness of this world,
against spiritual wickedness in high places.

Philippians 3:13

Brethren, I count not myself to have apprehended: but this one thing I
do, forgetting those things which are behind, and reaching forth unto
those things which are before ...

Philippians 3:14

I press toward the mark for the prize of the high calling of God in Christ
Jesus.

Philippians 4:13

I can do all things through Christ which strengtheneth me.

Colossians 3:1

If ye then be risen with Christ, seek those things which are above, where
Christ sitteth on the right hand of God.

2 Timothy 1:7

For God hath not given us the spirit of fear; but of power, and of love,
and of a sound mind.

2 Timothy 2:15–16

Study to shew thyself approved unto God, a workman that needeth not
to be ashamed, rightly dividing the word of truth.
But shun profane and vain babblings: for they will increase unto more
ungodliness.

Hebrews 1:1

God, who at sundry times and in divers manners spake in time past unto
the fathers by the prophets ...

Hebrews 8:6

But now hath he obtained a more excellent ministry, by how much also he is the mediator of a better covenant, which was established upon better promises.

Hebrews 9:2–6

For there was a tabernacle made; the first, wherein was the candlestick, and the table, and the shewbread; which is called the sanctuary.

And after the second veil, the tabernacle which is called the Holiest of all;

Which had the golden censer, and the ark of the covenant overlaid round about with gold, wherein was the golden pot that had manna, and Aaron's rod that budded, and the tables of the covenant;

And over it the cherubims of glory shadowing the mercyseat; of which we cannot now speak particularly.

Now when these things were thus ordained, the priests went always into the first tabernacle, accomplishing the service of God.

Hebrews 9:16

For where a testament is, there must also of necessity be the death of the testator.

Hebrews 10:23

Let us hold fast the profession of our faith without wavering; (for he is faithful that promised;)

Hebrews 10:28–29

He that despised Moses' law died without mercy under two or three witnesses:

Of how much sorer punishment, suppose ye, shall he be thought worthy, who hath trodden under foot the Son of God, and hath counted the blood of the covenant, wherewith he was sanctified, an unholy thing, and hath done despite unto the Spirit of grace?

Hebrews 10:35–36

Cast not away therefore your confidence, which hath great recompence of reward.

For ye have need of patience, that, after ye have done the will of God, ye might receive the promise.

Hebrews 11:1

Now faith is the substance of things hoped for, the evidence of things not seen.

Hebrews 11:6

But without faith it is impossible to please him: for he that cometh to God must believe that he is, and that he is a rewarder of them that diligently seek him.

Hebrews 12:2

Looking unto Jesus the author and finisher of our faith; who for the joy that was set before him endured the cross, despising the shame, and is set down at the right hand of the throne of God.

James 2:14

What doth it profit, my brethren, though a man say he hath faith, and have not works? can faith save him?

James 2:17

Even so faith, if it hath not works, is dead, being alone.

1 Peter 1:18

Forasmuch as ye know that ye were not redeemed with corruptible things, as silver and gold, from your vain conversation received by tradition from your fathers;

1 Peter 1:23

Being born again, not of corruptible seed, but of incorruptible, by the word of God, which liveth and abideth for ever.

2 Peter 2:4

For if God spared not the angels that sinned, but cast them down to hell, and delivered them into chains of darkness, to be reserved unto judgment ...

1 John 1:7

But if we walk in the light, as he is in the light, we have fellowship one with another, and the blood of Jesus Christ his Son cleanseth us from all sin.

1 John 1:9 King James Version (KJV)

If we confess our sins, he is faithful and just to forgive us our sins, and to cleanse us from all unrighteousness.

1 John 5:14–15

And this is the confidence that we have in him, that, if we ask any thing according to his will, he heareth us:
And if we know that he hear us, whatsoever we ask, we know that we have the petitions that we desired of him.

Jude 1:6

And the angels which kept not their first estate, but left their own habitation, he hath reserved in everlasting chains under darkness unto the judgment of the great day.

Revelation 1:5–6

And from Jesus Christ, who is the faithful witness, and the first begotten of the dead, and the prince of the kings of the earth. Unto him that loved us, and washed us from our sins in his own blood,

And hath made us kings and priests unto God and his Father; to him be
glory and dominion for ever and ever. Amen.

Revelation 1:7

Behold, he cometh with clouds; and every eye shall see him, and they also
which pierced him: and all kindreds of the earth shall wail because
of him. Even so, Amen.

Revelation 6:12–17

And I beheld when he had opened the sixth seal, and, lo, there was a great
earthquake; and the sun became black as sackcloth of hair, and the
moon became as blood;

And the stars of heaven fell unto the earth, even as a fig tree casteth her
untimely figs, when she is shaken of a mighty wind.

And the heaven departed as a scroll when it is rolled together; and every
mountain and island were moved out of their places.

And the kings of the earth, and the great men, and the rich men, and
the chief captains, and the mighty men, and every bondman, and
every free man, hid themselves in the dens and in the rocks of the
mountains;

And said to the mountains and rocks, Fall on us, and hide us from the
face of him that sitteth on the throne, and from the wrath of the
Lamb:

For the great day of his wrath is come; and who shall be able to stand?

Revelation 7:14

And I said unto him, Sir, thou knowest. And he said to me, These are
they which came out of great tribulation, and have washed their
robes, and made them white in the blood of the Lamb.

Revelation 9:2–4

And he opened the bottomless pit; and there arose a smoke out of the pit, as the smoke of a great furnace; and the sun and the air were darkened by reason of the smoke of the pit.

And there came out of the smoke locusts upon the earth: and unto them was given power, as the scorpions of the earth have power.

And it was commanded them that they should not hurt the grass of the earth, neither any green thing, neither any tree; but only those men which have not the seal of God in their foreheads.

Revelation 9:6

And in those days shall men seek death, and shall not find it; and shall desire to die, and death shall flee from them.

Revelation 16:14

For they are the spirits of devils, working miracles, which go forth unto the kings of the earth and of the whole world, to gather them to the battle of that great day of God Almighty.

Revelation 19:11

And I saw heaven opened, and behold a white horse; and he that sat upon him was called Faithful and True, and in righteousness he doth judge and make war.

Notes

Unless otherwise indicated, all scriptures are taken from the King James Version of the Bible (KJV).

Chapter 1
What Is Faith?
1. Frederick K. C. Price, DD, *Faith, Foolishness, or Presumption?* (Faith One Publishing), 1979.
2. Elder Shelia King, instructor, the Potter's Institute, Fall Term 1, *Faith* (Section/Course #:FCL1702-301, 2009).

Chapter 2
My Past and Faith
1. George Land, researcher, Creativity Test.
2. Smith Wigglesworth, *The Power of Faith*. New Kensington: (Whitaker House), 2000.

Chapter 3
Business and Faith (Passion and Profit)
1. Bishop T. D. Jakes, *The Live On Purpose*. Leadership Edition DVD Series.

Chapter 4

My Mom and Faith (Dementia/Alzheimer's)

1. *Wikipedia*, s.v. "neurodegeneration," https://en.wikipedia.org/wiki/Neurodegeneration.

Chapter 6

Family and Faith (Stop the Madness)

1. Jentezen Franklin, *Fasting*. Lake Mary: (Charisma House), 2008.

Chapter 7

Ministry and Faith (Just Have Faith)

1. *Merriam-Webster's Collegiate Dictionary*, 11th ed., Springfield, MA: (Merriam-Webster), 2003.
2. Dr. David Jeremiah, *Walking Down the Romans Road* (Quick Reference Guide for Sharing Your Faith).